DEVELOP
YOUR
MANAGEMENT
POTENTIAL

DEVELOP
YOUR
MANAGEMENT
POTENTIAL

A SELF-HELP GUIDE

John Coopey and
John Beech with
Charlotte Chambers
and Adrian McLean

SECOND EDITION

AMED

KOGAN
PAGE

First published in 1990
Reprinted 1994

Apart from any fair dealing for the purposes of research or private
study, or criticism or review, as permitted under the Copyright,
Designs and Patents Act, 1988, this publication may only be
reproduced, stored or transmitted, in any form or by any means,
with the prior permission in writing of the publishers, or in the case
of reprographic reproduction in accordance with the terms of
licences issued by the Copyright Licensing Agency. Enquiries
concerning reproduction outside those terms should be sent to the
publishers at the undermentioned address:

Kogan Page Limited
120 Pentonville Road
London N1 9JN

© Association for Management Education and Development
(AMED), 1993

British Library Cataloguing in Publication Data

A CIP record for this book is available from the British Library.

ISBN 0 7494 0971 1

Typeset by The Castlefield Press Ltd, Wellingborough, Northants.
Printed and bound in Great Britain by Clays Ltd, St Ives plc.

Contents

About the authors

The first edition of this book was written by Charlotte Chambers, John Coopey and Adrian Mclean. For this second edition John Beech has worked with John Coopey to make the necessary revisions with the support and encouragement of Charlotte and Adrian. We have all recently made major changes in our lives through decisions relating to our employment and work.

John Coopey moved about six years ago to Birkbeck College as a lecturer in Organisational Behaviour, after a career spent in employee relations management mainly in the oil industry. Two years ago he moved to Dundee University, teaching and researching in management.

John Beech worked until 1992 in a small training organisation dedicated to meeting the needs of the airline industry. Now he teaches management at a variety of levels at De Montfort University in Bedford.

Charlotte Chambers spent nearly twenty years in a management school before moving about six years ago to a management development position in a commercial organisation. More recently she has started with colleagues a consultancy, YSC, offering services in management and organisation development.

Adrian McLean left a business school some seven years ago to set up with partners a consultancy, Bath Associates, specialising in organisation development with a particular emphasis on culture. He is now a principal of McLean and George Consulting.

We all belong to the Association for Management Education and Development (AMED), where the need for the first edition of this book was identified following some initial work by John Coopey and Adrian McLean. AMED, whose aims and activities are described at the end of the book, has about 2000 members who are very well informed on the subject of personal and management development in the UK. Its events and publications may be of value to readers.

The book is dedicated to all those who contributed ideas at its inception and to those who, hopefully, will use it to enhance the quality of their own lives and of the communities in which they live.

Introduction

Background

This book is about the development of people as managers, and the question of improved practice. It is particularly addressed to managers who are concerned about their own capability and performance, but we hope it will also be of use to those people who have a professional interest in management development.

The need for the first edition of this book emerged following two major reports[1] on management education in the UK. These showed that British managers have far less formal education at higher levels and spend much less time in management education and development than managers in many equivalent countries. The reports prompted a considerable debate on management education and development, mostly around the question, 'How can we vastly increase the numbers of British managers who obtain management qualifications?'.

In the three years since the book was first published this question is still important, especially in the work of the council set up in response to the reports and of its successor organisation 'The Management Charter Initiative' (MCI). Many useful steps have been taken in defining managerial competences, establishing appropriate formal qualifications at various career stages, making formal study more relevant to the needs of practising managers and in allowing prior experience to be taken into account in assessing competence and awarding qualifications.

A sort of 'Good Beer Guide'

More important perhaps for the purpose of this book, the debate has moved on and widened considerably to take account of issues about which members of the Association for

Management Education and Development (AMED) have long been concerned. They and a growing body of people in the field feel that the focus on qualifications is too narrow and that the real key to having well developed managers lies in ensuring that the managers themselves are informed and discriminating about what is on offer and have a full understanding of what they can do for themselves. The analogy that emerged for us was the 'Good Beer Guide': we were inspired by the impressive accomplishment of the Campaign for Real Ale in forcing the breweries to rethink their policies as a result of the book's publication.

The analogy seemed just right: aiming to give more power to the consumer so as to ensure a better service. In beer terms this means getting the most out of drinking – how to tell a good from a bad brew; where to get the better brews; and, longer term, how to influence the brewers to provide a wider and improved choice.

But, not surprisingly, we soon found problems in translating from beer to management development! Most of us recognise a pint when we see one and can all too easily test a variety of them in a short period. We have our own tastes and preferences, developed by trying new brews and comparing notes with our drinking companions. And if we don't like what one pub has to offer we can just go somewhere else.

The general idea can be applied to management development: yes, we would like to make the best of our development opportunities just as we do of our drinking; and the same key question can be asked – are the consumer's needs being met? But 'needs' in management development are often ill-defined; and the idea of individual 'taste' is similarly difficult to pin down. People have different notions of what management and management development are. Even when taste is developed there are a variety of ways of satisfying it. What's more, development opportunities are not available on tap, to be savoured by moving from one experience to another in quick succession. And one crucial avenue for opening up choices – moving from one organisation to another – has its own pitfalls and traumas.

Unlike beer drinkers, managers have a special relationship with the major source of development experience – the organisation in which they work. There are other providers in the field – external management and business schools, consultants, counsellors, and so on – but by far the largest part of managers' development is likely to take place within their own organisation – and to be powerfully affected by whoever is their boss.

We therefore recognised that in affecting the perceptions of managers as consumers of management development, we might also help them to provide a fruitful environment for the development of their own subordinates.

Our hope, therefore, is that this book will help you and also that it will draw attention to managers as consumers, with rights as well as responsibilities regarding their development.

The time is right

Now is a good time for providing guidance. Until quite recently the demand for skilled technicians, professionals and managers generally exceeded the supply. For that reason many senior management teams developed a two-pronged strategy: of making their organisations more attractive to potential recruits and of enhancing the capability of existing employees through education, training and development. Frequently, the deep recession of the early 1990s has removed half of the rationale: rather than recruiting new employees, many organisations are making existing staff redundant, including professionals in larger numbers than ever before. But there is good news in that the senior managers of those enterprises which survive are more likely to realise the importance of developing their human resources, especially managers and others with management potential. In this context anyone wishing to change jobs, or to re-enter employment having been made redundant, needs to try harder than ever to develop their capabilities so as to enhance their attractiveness to potential employers. On the other hand, once in a job, it is quite probable that the employer will provide a wider range of opportunities than before for continuing that development process. We therefore believe that this book may make a contribution in opening up a debate between you and your employer and between managers more generally and those that provide management education and training.

In this early part of the book we refer to some of the controversies that have arisen recently about how best to provide for the development of competent managers. We will refer quite often to large organisations because it is here that most formal management development activity has taken place so far. We realise, however, that many managers work in smaller organisations where such development activities are less frequent and less formal. Do not, therefore, be put off by these references to the larger firm. The type of development we will be describing can be encouraged wherever managers work. And, increasingly, small and medium sized organisations are showing an interest in management development.

Defining our terms

We begin by addressing some basic and essential questions:

1. What do we understand by the term *management*?
2. How are we using the term *development*?
3. What do we mean by the terms *management* and *organisation development*?

What is management?

The meaning of the term management can be debated at length but, as our starting point, we offer the following thoughts on 'management' and 'managing'.

Management or managing?

The term management is used in two ways. Commonly it is used to refer to a class of people within an organisation – 'the management'. However, it is also used to describe a process, so that we sometimes talk about 'the management of our personal finances' or 'the management of our time'. A good deal of confusion has arisen from these two uses of the word. In the first case, we refer to a position within an organisation, sometimes connoting privilege and power; in the second we are dealing with a process, the accomplishment of a particular goal or intention through some form of organising, whether of people, ideas, materials or information.

The role of manager in this latter sense is very pervasive. When looked at in this way we can begin to understand all sorts of contradictions that lie at the heart of much cynical observation and comment in organisations. 'Calls himself a manager? He couldn't organise a bun-fight in a bakery!' – the implication being that management is the capacity to make intended and acceptable things happen through the use of given resources.

This guide is therefore not solely directed at those people who carry the formal title of 'manager' but is addressed to all who have responsibility for the process of managing, whatever their official label. Broadly, this includes people with responsibilities for others, for committing resources and for linking with the broader context of the organisation or environment.

In this sense then, management, or managing, is:

- a process requiring active doing and reflection.
- normally characterised by an element of stewardship or custody for a task, project, or group, and implies overall responsibility.
- concerned with achieving desired goals, perhaps the production of objects, information, or services. Sometimes this can mean maintaining an existing condition, say quality standards, safety or temperature in a building; or, it can also mean ensuring that a desired change is

accomplished: the 'business is turned around', or the service has been improved.

Managing in tougher situations

However, in recent years people have become increasingly aware that the process of making things happen in an effective way requires a great deal of skill and the situations in which people need to manage are becoming more extensive and much more demanding.

The process of managing is being pushed outwards from the top of organisations to people who would not have considered themselves managers in the past. This is happening for many reasons, including:

- Business is becoming more international.
- Commercial, economic, social and political climates are increasingly turbulent.
- Consumers are more demanding, prompted by Government-inspired charters of rights.
- Competitors create pressure for higher quality, lower cost and better service.
- Products and technologies are changing ever more quickly.
- New technologies bring new patterns of work and relationships.
- Information technology and management information systems produce masses of information for managerial use.
- In striving to meet these challenges organisations are tending to become more complex, with fewer formal levels of management, involving more employees in making judgments and decisions.

All this adds up to a constant pressure to change, adapt, respond and to try always to make the place in which we work more effective.

Changing ideas about good management

Management theorists and writers seeking to pin down

what 'good managers' should do identified typically such activities as planning, communicating, monitoring, motivating, and decision-making. More recently however, as researchers have monitored how senior managers *actually* spend their time, many of these prescriptions have had to be revised.

Managers, it is now realised, tend not to conduct orderly, well-planned lives, but tend to operate in a much more spontaneous, and often piece-meal way, scattering their attention and energy across many small tasks in a day and relying heavily on oral communication.[2] As a result there is a growing recognition of the need to define 'good management practice' more in terms of results or outcomes (within acceptable limits) than in terms of the methods and processes that are used to arrive at the outcomes.

In short, the emerging view is that there are many ways of being a 'good manager'. What counts is the extent to which individuals realise their full potential for managing.

What is development?

'Development' implies improvement, becoming more accomplished at doing things which help us to adapt to the environment we are living in now and to different ones we might have to contend with in the future. Development is the sign of intelligent activity resulting in increased knowledge, understanding, skills and judgment. In part these come through formal education and training but more crucial, in laying the foundation for learning, is the way we create and use experience. How much we learn and how quickly we develop depend on our willingness to experiment, to practise and reflect on the outcome; to question, to observe and listen; to challenge ourselves and others and to respond to challenges in turn. The essential question is how can we live our daily lives in ways that enhance our capacity to learn and adapt?

There are many strands to the debate about development,

some of which relate to specific issues such as competence, good practice, appropriate education and training programmes and types of formal qualification. We prefer to see development as being about more general and personal ques-tions concerned with preparedness, resourcefulness, enhanced capacities for responding and acting in a variety of settings, leading to an increased self knowledge and confidence.

Management development is therefore about helping an individual to realise his or her full potential for managing in a way that allows for the individuality of the person and which enhances effectiveness within a particular context.

This book is written in this spirit, and Part II will take you through a detailed process for examining and managing your own development.

Development for your current job

Development in this sense can mean the extension of understanding or abilities, such as how to read a profit and loss statement, or how to use a word processor, or how to make a presentation. You extend your repertoire of skills, abilities and knowledge but within a stable context, where the goals set for the job remain essentially the same.

Development in new work settings

Development can also refer to the ability to function competently in new arenas or at different levels, needing to cope with uncertainty and acquire a new set of skills and knowledge. It is often triggered by events, some of which are predictable such as promotions or attending courses, and some of which are quite unexpected, such as the loss of an account, a personal or organisational crisis, or perhaps suddenly being 'thrown in at the deep end'.

This second type of development can be illustrated by the difference between being trained as a supervisor in a bank and becoming a bank manager. It involves more than just a larger number of responsibilities; the whole quality of the job is different. It entails shifting quickly to a different level and area of performance, where old skills and competences, however fully developed and well performed, may be of little direct relevance. Most typically when people move from a job requiring technical expertise to a more general management role with wider responsibilities, a different form of development is called for.

Given the rate at which organisations and their contexts are changing, this second type of development can now often be required even when you don't change jobs. Organisations can move from a seemingly steady state to crisis overnight with demands on managers becoming completely different.

We use the term development, then, in two different but equally important ways:

- to represent the extension of skills and competence within an established domain of work-life;
- to describe the acquisition of skills and understanding appropriate to accomplished performance in a new sphere of work.

Management development is concerned with both these forms.

Management development as a bridge between the individual and the organisation

It is easy to assume that management development is concerned with the development of individuals and forget that, at its best, it also contributes to the development of the organisation. It is about both at the same time.

Development activities can either be very specific and limited, such as instruction in the use of a particular procedure or system, or they can have far-reaching effects that can change people's lives or shape strategic policy formation.

When viewed in this way, it becomes possible to represent

management development as a connection between the individual and the organisation which has the potential to influence both profoundly. This is illustrated in Figure 1.

On the individual's side, management development can contribute to the extension of technical skills, abilities and knowledge (level 1). At a higher level it may help the manager adapt to a whole new arena of activity or performance (level 2). Finally, at level 3, it can provide opportunities for major personal insights and growth that influence the whole way of life; repercussions extend well beyond the organisational arena.

On the organisational side of the picture, the benefits of management development at level 1 are that managers become adequately trained and knowledgeable to perform their tasks competently. For example, they can prepare and monitor a budget.

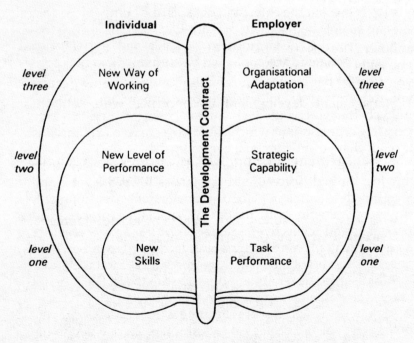

Figure 1   *Individual and employer concerns about management development*

At level 2, management development is linked to the implementation of corporate policy. It exists within a strategic developmental framework derived from the ambitions of the organisation as a whole – for instance, where a company realises that it must enhance the overall levels of market understanding throughout management.

Finally, level 3 is where management development is so tailored as to feed into and influence the nature and quality of corporate policy forming processes. Not only are the management development activities shaped by the overall goals and direction of the business but they also exercise an influence over these matters.

We suggest that management development activities and processes represent a vital means through which the realms of personal and organisational development needs can be reconciled.

Obviously, people and organisations need to be matched in some way that enables them to meet their expectations of one another. Thus, if work plays a very small part in your life and you want to concentrate your energy entirely on other areas, you may be happiest in an organisation which only expects you to learn a new skill every two or three years. It is most unlikely that you would be in a managerial job, and there are very few organisations which could now survive with this low level of change and personal commitment.

So, in reality, both individuals and organisations seem to be moving through force of circumstances toward level 2 and level 3 development. Good management development, therefore, benefits both parties by facilitating processes of personal and collective adaptation. The actual level of development appropriate for you is likely to depend on both your starting point and what pressures exist for adaptation. But for us good development doesn't stop there: like it or not there is also an ethical dimension.

At a time when we are beginning to acknowledge the political, social and ecological catastrophies perpetrated in the name of 'development', those of us in Management Development are compelled to ask ourselves: 'development for what'?

In particular we need to be mindful of the consequences of 'development' thinking on the lives of less privileged people both in industrialised societies and the Third World.

At the level of organisations and their management these concerns are being voiced about a host of pressing issues: threats to the environment; corporate ethics and the governance of organisations; giving people a chance to adapt to change rather than 'throwing them on the scrap heap' in a drive for efficiency; the regulation of financial markets to safeguard fraud; and the position of 'whistle blowers' who draw public attention to unethical behaviour on the part of corrupt or dishonest officials.

We are interested in development which helps us and our organisations to adapt in ways which will contribute to a better world — in a physical, social and spiritual sense. We need to question whether development will enhance our pride in our behaviour as managers and in the practices of the organisations for which we work. This might entail forfeiting short-term personal rewards or corporate profits in order to do the right rather than the expedient thing.

Even here there is a parallel with the 'Good Beer Guide'. Do we go to the pub just to get drunk, with all of the consequences this might entail — hangover, diminished work performance, bad temper, driving offences, battered partners and children? Or do we hope to enjoy in company the taste of our favourite ale, revelling in the freeing of ideas and feelings which it can bring, and sharing in the social warmth created by mutual enjoyment?

So, is it to be development for its own sake, just a means to whatever ends offer themselves? Or — as we hope, without apology — should it lead if possible to a better life in the fullest sense for ourselves, the organisation and the wider community of which all are part?

The development contract

As represented in the central area of Figure 1 the process of adjustment between individuals and their need for stretch and growth, and the organisation and its need for development and adaptation, results in some sort of contract, even if this is never made explicit. So, for instance, you go to a particular organisation because of its reputation for providing challenging and developmental work experience and they choose you partly because you seem to be hungry for the opportunity to learn. If it turns out that the organisation is not able to provide the development you thought it would, you are likely to feel that it is not fulfilling its side of the contract and you may seek other opportunities inside or outside the organisation. Similarly, if it turns out that you are unwilling or unable to learn and grow at the pace the organisation expects, then the organisation is unlikely to continue to provide developmental opportunities and may in time either push you into a side-track or encourage you to leave.

The notion of a development contract can form the basis of a specific development agreement between the individual and the organisation. This theme is developed further at the end of the Chapter and in Part II.

What is managerial competence?

A major issue in the debate we referred to earlier has been concerned with what managers need in order to be competent in their jobs. It may seem strange that this has emerged as a serious widespread concern only recently, rather than at the time when the Business Schools were developing in the 1960s. However, dissatisfaction had been expressed for some considerable time within organisations and among managers. They were critical of the emphasis that many of the schools placed upon conceptual knowledge and analytical techniques and of the relative lack of apparent concern for practical managerial capability. These features may have accounted in part for the relatively low proportion of managers in the UK who undertook formal management education.

Over the last few years there has therefore been discussion

and research both within organisations and also within the academic world, to try and show what competence a manager must possess to do a good job. The debate is a complicated one but, not surprisingly, seems to reveal that although there are some very basic common skills, managers in different organisations have to learn things appropriate to that organisation.

It is important that you know what people mean when they talk about 'competence' or 'competences' because you will find that the ideas and the terminology pop up all over the place when management education and development and managerial performance are being discussed.

At the simplest level, the competence (or competences) required can be a fragmented list of skills, knowledge, and personal characteristics, that are identified by those in charge as necessary for a manager in a particular job at a particular time. There are also general lists of skills and characteristics which have been developed through research with large populations of managers.

At a more elaborate level, what constitutes competence may be based on investigations within an organisation which lead to a better understanding of what specific capabilities have tended to be associated with high levels of managerial performance in the recent past and which lead to a productive debate about future requirements for managing.

Obviously, both of these approaches tend to improve the understanding of the link between development and management performance. However, the simple approach is likely to be quickly outgrown in any organisation which is serious about the development of its management capability.

If the diagnosis of development needs rests with people in senior positions the learner managers may have no sense of ownership of, and responsibility for, their own development. This may work well in situations where many people are appointed to their first and perhaps second managerial job in quite similar contexts and where there is a lot of appropriate experience at a senior level about how best to do these jobs. In these cases, it makes sense to systematise this accumulated experience for the benefit of new managers. This approach, however, tends to emphasise the static elements of the job rather than exploring areas of change, friction and mismatch. It will not automatically lead to any real understanding by managers of how to identify what they need to learn and how best to learn it.

If, however, the identification of what makes a person competent in a particular job is explored jointly between the job holder and the boss or someone who is helping in the development, the outcome will be quite different. Job holders are likely to gain real understanding of the connection between how they perform as managers and what capability or competence they need to have. This is likely to have a considerable impact on motivation to learn.

The 'top-down' approaches are therefore best suited to large, relatively bureaucratic organisations in the few sectors which change relatively slowly and smoothly. They will tend to be inappropriate in smaller organisations where each job is different and the rate of change is high.

The great benefit that is likely to come from the discussion of competence is that many of those providing management development are having to look much more closely at their programmes to ensure that they emphasise improved managerial performance as a necessary outcome and not just rigorous academic understanding or the latest trendy training technique.

However, you need to assess whether the term is being used to generate a productive debate on what capability is needed and how it might best be acquired, or whether it is being used as a prescriptive formula aimed at making you fit into a particular organisational mould.

For business and management schools, for organisations and for individual managers who want to develop themselves, it is almost certainly useful to focus on competence rather than just knowledge, so long as it is recognised that this is only part of what development is all about and that it is unlikely that any list of competences is going to be appropriate for all young managers.

Development can be messy! – Learning from experience

As you can see, there is a danger of assuming that management development is concerned with the tidy and predictable outcomes of structured events and activities; that management development is 'what you go on courses for'.

While the main vehicle used for management development has traditionally been courses, much current practice recognises and tries to include the much broader, and at times messier, arena of daily experiences within organisations, which is increasingly seen as a more important source of development. The increasing use of project groups, action learning sets and self-managed learning initiatives within organisations reflect this shift in thinking.

Beyond these approaches, however, we recognise a third, broad arena in which development occurs and over which professional developers have no direct control whatsoever. It is the arena in which opportunities occur often in dramatic and unwanted form.

Learning from failures

This is when you encounter the unintended, the disaster, the personal or organisational catastrophe of redundancy or bankruptcy. Management development in such circumstances can promote learning from the experience. To benefit from such painful episodes, including failures, is every bit as important as learning from a course or less structured form of development.

In this book we are viewing management development in the broadest of senses. We see it as *the capacity to incorporate learnings into behaviour* in a way which is appropriate to the setting and the changes in the situation and to the desired outcomes in those settings. It is concerned with the incorporation of learnings from all arenas into the individual's daily organisational life. The success of management development can only be judged through the action and behaviour of people.

Management and organisation development

The term 'organisation development' is often used alongside management development. Frequently the two complement each other. Ideally management development policies and practices are designed to fit into an overall strategy for the development of the organisation as a whole. This is not always the case, however.

So as to understand the differences between the two and the effects of each on the other, we briefly set out what the term organisation development means, and describe the types of activities it involves.

Organisation development is concerned with enhancing the capabilities and operation of an organisation as a whole. The term was first used in the 1960s when people saw the need for organisations to be more adaptable and flexible in response to accelerating technological, commercial, and social changes. Organisation development draws on a wide variety of approaches that require organisation members to take a broader view of their activities and to address some of the problems that can easily undermine corporate effectiveness.

Typically, members of organisations, especially as they grow, can find it difficult to think in corporate terms, as they become preoccupied with the immediate needs and pressing concerns of their own department or section. Sometimes unhealthy rivalries develop between departments and, as a consequence, the customer suffers poor service. Sometimes organisations become complacent and insensitive to competitors and their products so that their own practices fall badly behind.

Although the phrase 'organisation development' has been less in use in the 80s than in the 60s and 70s, it describes a body of ideas and practices that still serve to help people recognise some of the difficulties their organisations face and to take steps to overcome them in the following ways:

- Developing corporate missions and visions.
- Developing effectiveness within working teams.

- Working to improve effectiveness between teams and departments.
- Reviewing and shaping the values and beliefs within the organisation – its culture.
- Designing organisation structures that support its primary goals and operations.

Good development – what is it?

Obviously, there can be no hard and fast rules which will characterise what is 'good' for any individual or any organisation. However, we have discussed the ideas we will present in this section extensively with those who have long and varied experience in the development and education of managers and we invite you to consider their value for you personally and for your organisation. We encourage you to read them critically, to reject those you don't agree with and to incorporate your own amendments.

We also invite you to comment on and debate these ideas with us, with providers you work with, and with fellow managers, since we believe that these are important issues that merit full debate.

Idealism or aspiration?

We propose these ideas in the full realisation that they appear high-minded and idealistic and that, while wholeheartedly embraced as proper and commonplace in some organisations, they may seem unrealistic, naïve and ambitious when compared to actual practice in others. Our concern here is not to provide a mirror of whatever developmental practices are considered normal or even realistic in your organisation, but to propose some yardsticks against which we can review current practice, debate the appropriateness of the yardsticks themselves, and consciously hold ourselves to account.

In our view, good development is characterised by the following features:

- You feel in control of the process. You do not feel bulldozed or bullied. You are an active and equal party to the process of identifying your development needs and deciding what is right for you.
- You receive active support from your colleagues and your supervisor as you need it based on the right to receive direct and open feedback about your performance.
- It is relevant to your needs, as you experience them, and is not imposed on you against your will or because it is considered to be 'good' for you.
- It recognises you as a complete, thinking and feeling person, and is relevant to your overall sense of yourself, not just the part of you involved in work.
- It assumes that you are part way along a journey, that you have already learned and developed a great deal, and that you will continue to do so.
- It takes account of the likelihood that your needs will change at different stages of your career and phases of your life. In this sense, good development is sensitive and responsive to your own personal lifestyle and emerging needs.
- It is about supporting you through difficult and challenging phases of your career and life, and encouraging constructive reflection, experimentation and learning.
- There is a climate of curiosity, challenge and questioning which asks: 'How can this be improved on? How can we learn from this experience, and how can we do it better next time?'
- There is an environment that encourages learning from experience, through reflection and feedback.

Finally, let us hope that good development defined in this way leads to lives that would give pleasure to obituary writers, to organisational records from which historians would be able to draw up very positive human balance sheets, and to wider communities within which all would be proud to be members.

Key responsibilities

These features of good development are not on tap like a fine ale, a pint ready to be pulled and quaffed. They must be provided by the key parties who collaborate in the process: the manager, the employer and other providers of developmental experience. In our view they have separate but complementary responsibilities as set out here.

The manager

The individual manager must take responsibility for his or her own development. Organisations are very much less permanent than they used to be and very few people can or would now expect to spend their whole career with one employer. Under these circumstances you are the only really reliable and continuous element in your own development and only for you are your own personal concerns central. We, therefore, suggest that you should:

- Reflect periodically on career objectives and learning to date, developing some overall sense of what you wish to achieve through your career. The purpose is to sustain some view of the types of opportunities you wish to pursue and the type of life you would be proud to live.
- Make yourself open to opportunities for learning, from both structured and unstructured sources. This is likely to entail taking risks and making yourself vulnerable.
- Seek out actively the support and guidance necessary for your own development.
- Create your own support group with whom it is safe to review the learnings from your experiences.
- Declare your needs and be prepared to negotiate for them.
- Make the most of the opportunities offered.

The organisation

Organisations claiming to provide good quality management development should:

- Offer or provide for all managers development opportunities arising from structured settings, structured processes, and unplanned events, allowing them to take risks.
- Help managers realise what choices are available for their development.
- Sanction time and resources for managers to engage in developmental activities. A reasonable level would probably be somewhere between five and ten days per year, depending upon the stage of career and rate of organisational change.
- Provide expert resources to create development activities and processes.
- Develop explicit, regularly reviewed contracts with each individual in respect of their development needs and how these may be met with organisational support during a specific time period.
- Ensure that management development policy is compatible with and contributing to corporate and strategic objectives.
- Foster a climate in which the processes of reflecting on action and continual learning are considered legitimate and normal.
- State clearly the limits of the organisation's responsibility for development and set out its expectations of the personal responsibilities of individuals for their own learning.

The provider of management development activities and courses

Those in the 'business' of management education and development are broadly of three types – those who work in management and business schools and colleges; those who operate as management development consultants; and those who work in companies as tutors, trainers, counsellors and designers of development activity. We believe their responsibility is to:

- Recognise that managers have a wealth of understanding, able to benefit from new perspectives, not empty buckets to be filled with expert knowledge.
- Act on the assumption that most managers can learn at least as much from one another as from a tutor, and show this in the methods of learning, the construction of groups and the timetabling of programmes.
- Show that they understand that individuals learn in different ways, provide opportunities to match these preferences and give advice that respects individual need rather than the need to sell places on courses.
- Ensure that managers with whom they come into contact gain insight into ways of learning as well as the content of what they learn. Tutors should be ready to explain any underlying techniques that they use to achieve particular learning objectives.
- Always listen to what their client is asking for and never assume that the ready-made package which worked for someone else is going to be appropriate.
- Keep closely in touch with their clients, their area of study and the changing environment.
- Review regularly the relevance of their skills, the value of their consultancy and research to their other work, and the design and range of their activities.
- Show in their work that they know that the world is not made up of 'subject areas', and find ways to re-integrate their understanding and the activities they undertake.
- Support both analysis and intuition in managers. Avoid the impression that theoretical models explain the whole of reality.
- Ensure that managers learn to evaluate situations from many perspectives and not just from that of the chief executive.
- Obtain feedback systematically not only on their performance as tutors but on their effect on learning and management capability. This is likely to involve a much longer-term assessment by their clients.
- Give feedback to individuals they meet whenever they are asked to do so.

• Recognise and respect the confidentiality of the information they acquire through their working relationships.

Development agreements

Earlier we mentioned the development contract, often implicit, which reflects the expectations the employer and the individual have of one another. Some organisations are beginning to make these expectations much more explicit by encouraging employees, particularly in jobs which require a lot of skill and know-how, to enter into personal development agreements with their immediate boss. Further details of this process are given on page 123, but, in brief, the agreements outline what areas of a person's performance or future activities need developing, how that will be done and with what support, and what standards will be reached by when.

This process clarifies the responsibilities of each side and is likely to lead to a more imaginative approach to the means of development than the usual 'training needs analysis', which tends merely to end up with 'What course can they be sent on?'.

We believe that these development agreements should become part of the routine process of ensuring that the individual and the organisation continuously recognise the need to learn, develop and adapt.

The rest of the book

Part II takes you through a fairly detailed process to help you review yourself and your work environment so that you can assess what is right for you.

Part III looks at courses, particularly qualification courses, and helps you to evaluate them in terms of relevance and quality.

Part IV gives you a glossary of terms that you may come

across – the management development jargon which can so easily be offputting.

At the end of the book is a list of agencies which can give you further advice and help, and a brief list of reading that you may find useful.

Notes

1. Handy, C B (1987) *The Making of Managers*, London: BIM and CBI. Constable, J and McCormick, R (1987) *The Making of British Managers*, London: NEDO.
2. Mintzberg, H (1973) *The Nature of Managerial Work*, New York: Harper & Row.

Part II Personal Review and Planning

Chapter 1
Introduction

In this part of the book, Chapters 2 and 3 prompt you to review aspects of your managerial experience and of the personal resources you bring to your work. In Chapter 4, you are encouraged to place any conclusions reached from these reviews within a life-career setting as a basis for making a personal development plan. The final chapter looks ahead to situations in which you might create opportunities to implement parts of that plan and to take advantage of opportunities provided by others, especially the organisation for which you work.

Although a specific route is set out through the various themes and issues introduced in the text it is up to you to decide how you make use of it. You might:

- work through the themes in the order set out
- create your own route through all the items covered
- concentrate only on those items of immediate interest
- decide not to respond to the prompts at all but just read this part of the book as a standard form of text. If so we hope that you still find the contents of interest and value.

How to use the text

You can decide how to use the text by skimming through the next four chapters paying most attention to their introductions and the preambles to each of the themes covered. If you do decide to work through all or some of the steps systematically we suggest that you:

- start a workbook, preferably loose-leaf so that it can easily be expanded or changed in sequence as your ideas and proposals for action develop.
- follow the prompts at each step to make notes of your responses to the questions raised and to carry forward a summary of the main conclusions as input to any personal

development plan you might make at the end of Chapter 4.
- Find a close friend, with whom you can discuss freely matters that arise in working through this part of the book. This should help you to interpret issues more clearly and to put them into a broader framework. We shall refer to this person as 'your friend'.

In many self-help books, there is a neat checklist of things to do that you can score. The implication is that if you go through these steps, all will be well. However, we do not believe that this simplistic approach can be used in something as complicated and important as your own life.

In the previous section, we emphasised that development can be messy. A simple checklist is certainly not going to make a difference in taking charge of your own development. The results of your work in this part will raise difficult and inconclusive issues. This is why your friend will be important in helping you to identify and resolve these issues. Once they are clearer you can then discuss them with other people who might be able to help in various ways.

Through the process of examining critically your experience and personal resources and of projecting your ideas forward, we are confident that you will be able to draft out a useful personal development plan. If you and we have done our work well the outcome will be:

- Improved insights into yourself as a person and as a manager.
- Better use of known development opportunities and the creation of new ones.
- Some outline of your longer term future as a person and as a manager.

Chapter 2
A Review of Experience

In this chapter we prompt you to reflect on your experience as a manager from the following seven perspectives:

(A) *Functional and General Management Experience* (p 39) – a review of your career to date as a functional specialist or general manager as an aid to deciding what sort of openings to look for when you next consider changing jobs.

(B) *Preferred Managerial Roles* (p 42) – examining your preferences among ten roles which typically occur within managerial jobs as a starting point for considering your self-image as a manager.

(C) *Responsibilities and Skills* (p 44) – emphasising your current job responsibilities, and the skills you need to discharge them.

(D) *Shaping the Role* (p 46) – shaping your role and the way this is done through relationships with subordinates, bosses, and peers.

(E) *Handling Differences of Values* (p 50) – reflecting on your own values and how they interact with those held widely within the organisation.

(F) *Managerial Power* (p 56) – examining the central part power plays in organisations, how much power you have, and how you feel about its use.

(G) *Political Awareness and Skills* (p 59) – exploring the political skill with which you act within the organisation.

Each section consists of four main parts:

* A preamble setting out the main points introduced and any special advice on working through the section. The key part is in bold, italic text for easy reference.
* A narrative section explaining the nature of the perspective.
* A series of questions or things you might do, with or without other prompts. Each question or suggestion is introduced with this symbol: ➤.

• A reminder to write up your answers to the questions and, after discussion with your friend, to carry forward a summary of any conclusions to use at the planning stage in Chapter 4.

In several of the sections, and again in Chapters 3 to 5, we introduce into the narrative illustrations based on a number of characters known by the authors. One of these, Neil Compton, appears from time to time throughout this part of the book, so we introduce him now in Box 1.

Box 1

NEIL COMPTON

Neil is 33, a product marketing manager with a small company, 'Planet Systems', which specialises in computer software used in project planning. This is the third company for which Neil has worked since leaving Southampton University 11 years ago. It was there that he became interested in computing while using the university computer extensively in a final-year Geography project. Neil worked first for a medium-sized computer manufacturer, 'Matrix Computers', with whom he stayed for three and a half years. There he gained his first management experience, running a small computer bureau. His next company, ICM, much smaller but growing rapidly, manufactures a range of computer communications equipment. Neil stayed there for five and a half years in various managerial and non-managerial roles concerned with software. He joined his present company in October 1990. With them Neil is continuing a part-time MBA at a university business school which was sponsored initially by his previous employer.
  The list of his job experience is:

MATRIX COMPUTERS
Sept 1981   Software support engineer
Nov 1983   Computer bureau supervisor
ICM
March 1985   Customer services telephone support manager
March 1986   Various customer services roles
Dec 1988   Product engineering manager

PLANET SYSTEMS
Oct 1990   Product marketing manager

(A) Functional and general management experience

In this first section you are asked to review the jobs you have done in your career to date as a starting point for deciding what sort of openings you might seek when next you consider a job move.

Start by listing in your workbook the organisations you have worked in and the jobs you have done in them, with dates, in the way shown for Neil Compton. (In Chapter 4 we will ask you to use this data again in preparing a life-career chart.)

(i) Moving across

Some people make successful managerial careers within one functional department such as production, sales, research and development and personnel or, say, a specialist department in a local authority. Others progress through a variety of different functions. A survey of a large sample of managers was completed a few years ago and described in a recent book[1] (throughout this part we will refer to this survey regularly simply as the 'Managerial Survey'). The managers sampled reported an average of about three years in a job. Neil Compton has had six jobs in almost eleven years so his average length of time in any one job is well below that of the sample. Perhaps the computer industry is particularly frenzied!

Some organisations positively encourage a broad portfolio of functional experience for their potential senior managers. This makes sense because general managers need to be able to resolve differences of interest between functions. Even at a lower level of management, those with experience of several functions should be better able to collaborate with colleagues in different departments.

Since this is a fairly practical issue which most managers will have considered from time to time it seemed to us a good place to start a review. Certainly Neil Compton has done this.

Because his first nine years' experience were largely in software systems support and development he deliberately chose to look for a new job in marketing – hence his current job as product marketing manager. Neil made this move even though he had reservations about the values that seemed to him to pervade sales and marketing. For example, when in systems support roles Neil had often been appalled at the willingness of computer industry marketers to push insufficiently tested and developed products. Now he's beginning to share the pressures on them while hoping not to succumb to expediency.

So let's start with a few questions (and if you propose to work through this part of the book systematically we suggest you start writing the answers down in your workbook so that a summary can be made and carried forward to the planning stage in Chapter 4):

➤ If you work in a specialised function within an organisation, how satisfied are you with the experience gained so far? What can you do to make up for any shortcomings? Are there other fields within the function you might wish to work in? How are you going to arrange that?

➤ Do you feel the need for other functional experience? If so, is there one function more than others which might broaden your experience quickly in line with your interests and needs?

There may be one function which is clearly dominant in your organisation in the sense that senior managers tend to be drawn from that department.

➤ Have you worked in that department? Or do you plan to do so? If not, how do you feel about cutting yourself off from an important potential route to career progression? (We are not implying that your choice may be wrong: only that you should be aware of the implications when you make that choice.)

Many organisations make plans for filling key management

jobs (called 'succession plans' – see Glossary and Chapter 5 for more details).

➤ Are you aware of such a plan in your organisation? If so, does it imply some 'ideal' set of functional management experiences which someone should have had on the way to a general manager position? If you don't know, how can you find out? Then, how does your experience match the ideal?

(ii) Moving up

You may have professional experience within a particular function and feel that you are now able to take on a managerial role in that function. Or you may feel ready to take on more general, cross-functional managerial responsibilities. Perhaps your recent performance appraisals have given you this impression.

➤ How might you check this out? What processes exist which are open to you to apply for consideration? Or is it a question of making your expectations known in some less formal way? In any case how are you going to do it without treading on people's toes?

Your early experience may have been out in the field as a manager of a small, self-contained unit such as a shop or sales area. If so,

➤ Do you want and expect to move beyond this? And how are you proposing to do it?

One route is to get 'stepping-stone' specialist experience within a function such as accounting or personnel, in your present organisation or elsewhere. Or it may be that the best way is to move on to manage a similar but bigger unit. If so,

➤ What do you need to do to prepare yourself and to engineer the desired change?

You may already be finding that it is not possible, at least yet, to answer some of these questions. Don't despair! First, remember to try to find a friend with whom you can discuss the thoughts you have had and any notes made so far, however confused they might seem. Merely trying to explain the issues to someone is a fairly sure way of clarifying things. Second, we will be returning to various aspects of these questions in the chapters that follow. So if what we have said so far has not helped you directly, make notes in your workbook of any provisional conclusions or outstanding questions which you can carry forward to the planning stage. And, finally, don't forget that we are not offering a 'quick fix': development is a life-long process and some of the issues may refuse to die until you do!

(B)   Preferred managerial roles

Now you are invited to consider which you prefer, if any, of a range of possible managerial roles

Henry Mintzberg's[2] review of a thirty-year stream of research studies into what managers actually do resulted in a list of managerial roles. As we discussed in Part I, unlike the conventional, earlier view of the manager as some sort of detached, reflective controller of subordinate performance, the findings summarised by Mintzberg show that managers' jobs are made up of activities which are brief, varied, and fragmented. Managers tend to gravitate toward the more active elements of their work – current, specific, well-defined and non-routine. Pressures on the manager encourage adaptive, manipulative and active behaviour rather than reflection and planning.

Despite this, Mintzberg claims that the research reveals a set of ten typical managerial roles, listed in Box 2. You may already have had the opportunity to try out some of these roles. If so,

➤ List them in your workbook and score each of them from 0 (did not enjoy doing) to 5 (enjoyed very much) and from A (did not do very well) to E (did very well indeed).

➤ Where you have not had the opportunity to try the roles, score 0 to 5 according to how much you would *expect* to enjoy them.

Add a few comments to each score to discuss with your friend. In this way you might sort out your preferences more clearly and obtain some insights into your self-image as a manager. Ask what it is about your personality, skills and values which causes you to have this view of yourself.

Once you have discussed the answers and comments with your friend, make a summary note as necessary to carry forward.

Box 2

TEN TYPICAL MANAGERIAL ROLES

Henry Mintzberg claims to have identified ten roles which, from his and other researchers' studies, seemed to appear most frequently in descriptions of managers' work. Three of these are about dealing with people, three with information, and four with decisions. They are summarised below:

Task	Description
Interpersonal:	
Figurehead	Performs symbolic duties of a legal or social nature
Leader	Motivates subordinates; carries out staffing, training, and related duties
Liaison	Maintains self-developed external network of contacts who provide favours and information
Informational:	
Monitor	Focuses on current internal and external information which makes him the 'nerve centre' for some part of the organisation
Disseminator	Interprets, integrates and transmits information received from internal and external network to members of the organisation

Spokesman	Transmits information on various aspects of organisation to outsiders
Decisional:	
Entrepreneur	Discovers opportunities inside and outside the organisation so as to initiate and perhaps supervise projects to bring about improved organisational performance
Disturbance handler	Takes corrective action to handle disturbance and crises
Resource allocator	Allocates organisational resources of all kinds through control of significant decisions
Negotiator	Conducts major negotiations with outsiders

(C) Responsibilities and skills

We now focus on the job you are doing currently and prompt you to question what sort of skills and knowledge you might consider developing.

Our perspective is based on responsibilities over various time-scales developed by John Kotter from detailed observations of what managers actually do.[3]

(i) Short-term

In the short-term, managers generally have to be able to handle a large range of activities and demands. They must spot problems quickly and be able to take rapid action to solve them. In this context:

➤ You are asked to make a list of the typical activities that you have to handle in a week.

Then respond to the following questions:

➤ What problems have you faced in the last month, and did you spot them soon enough?

➤ Could you have done better at spotting and solving the problems?

➤ What sort of skills and knowledge do you need to acquire or to improve in order to handle the tasks and to spot and solve problems effectively?

(ii) *Medium-term*

In the medium-term, managers often need to decide how to employ resources that they control (eg people's time, money, equipment) in the most effective way to achieve the established goals. This means keeping a balance between short-run issues and the long run and between the concerns and pressures that come from different groups — other departments, customers and clients, trade unions, and so on. In this setting:

➤ the resources you control or can influence.

Then answer these questions:

➤ Do you know exactly how they are being used?

➤ What new or improved skills or knowledge do you need in order to ensure that the resources are used better?

(iii) *Longer-term*

Managers also have to set longer-range goals for their part of the organisation. They have to be ready to handle considerable uncertainty arising from areas outside their control, like the state of the economy, new or revised government regulations, or just the way other departments or competitors are behaving. The more senior the manager the more crucial these longer-term goals are likely to be.

➤ Do you know what the longer-term goals of the whole organisation are, and your part in their achievement?

➤ Are you clear about what strategies you would need to adopt to get there?

➤ Do you have sufficient information from which to

determine the longer-term options open to you in following those strategies?

➤ What skills and knowledge do you need to enhance or to acquire in order to develop strategies and analyse your options within the limits of those strategies?

Note down your skills and knowledge action points from each of the time-scales and discuss them with your friend as necessary. Try to prioritise any proposals and carry forward a summary of the most important of them to the planning stage.

(D) Shaping the role

Here we consider how you shape your role through your relationships with subordinates, bosses and peers.

There is more to a manager's role than these time-related activities or lists of items like those produced by Mintzberg. What is more, the tasks managers undertake and the behaviours expected of them are not clearly defined in the way that, say, an auditor's might be.

In effect, a manager's role emerges from the interaction of four factors:

(i)   Any job description, operating procedures or contractual agreements which place limits on possible behaviour.
(ii) The preferences, or expectations, of the manager concerned.
(iii) Personal qualities, skills and competences.
(iv) The expectations of those with whom the manager must work to fulfil the role.

Other people's expectations are crucial. The expectations of the boss are naturally very formative; but your immediate peers and subordinates, too, will have expectations that you neglect at your peril. Then there are colleagues in other units of the organisation, external contacts, family members, various close friends and mentors, etc.

In some situations, the expectations of one key person or group may be incompatible with those of another. Or there may be several conflicting roles within a job so that you find that if you are playing one, eg 'obedient subordinate', you find it difficult to play 'assertive boss' also. If the range of roles you have to play is too great, you may feel hopelessly overloaded; or at the other extreme, people may expect so little of you that there just isn't enough challenge. And many roles are ambiguous, a situation which can cause considerable uncertainty and anxiety.

Each of these role difficulties and the way you deal with them can cause levels of role stress which are damaging to your performance, and possibly health. The symptoms may be tension (shown for example by irritability, sensitivity to criticism and periods of sickness, etc), low morale, and difficulties in communication with colleagues. Conversely role difficulties may be seen as opportunities. Ambiguity can allow scope for you to shape the role to suit your preferences. Incompatibility of role expectations can be exploited too, while a lack of challenge may provide scope and time to 'branch out' to find or develop something more interesting. This is just what Neil Compton did when he joined Planet Systems only to find that the project he had been recruited to market had been deferred!

Opportunities of this sort probably account for why, despite potential role difficulties, most managers have some freedom to adapt their role – perhaps by modifying its purpose, but more probably its content. This was true even in the larger, more bureaucratic organisations sampled in the Managerial Survey, although it was found that smaller organisations seemed to provide greater scope for managers to shape their roles.

A significant proportion of the 2000 managers surveyed reported considerable opportunity to modify their roles on change of job. Over 30% said, for example, that they approached their job 'very differently' to other people in respect of setting objectives, deciding methods to be used, deciding the order of tasks, and choosing with whom to deal in the role. Important for us is the finding that those who managed to shape their roles in this way felt that this experience had helped in their personal growth and development.

Crucial in determining the scope you have to shape your role is the way you handle relationships with those around you: subordinates, bosses and peers. So let's concentrate on and question these relationships.

(i) Downward relationships

These are often described in terms of 'motivating and controlling subordinates'. Yet the 'mirror image' can be very different. Many of those sampled in the Managerial Survey, for example, reported disappointment with their own managers and supervisors. The latter did not meet their subordinates' high expectations – that they would acquire the resources needed, provide personal support, publicise their group's achievements, deflect criticism, and so on.

Since the focus of our book is your development as a manager and, therefore, the development of the people who report to you, the perspective we prefer to use can be summed up in this way:

➤ What are you doing or going to do to help them become more motivated and autonomous?

This puts the onus on them to control their own activities and outputs, leaving you to manage the boundaries upwards with your bosses and sideways with peers. Of course there will be cases of inadequate performance and of conflicts between members of your group which you will need to tackle directly. But there are plenty of 'how to do it' books and other sources of advice on problems of this sort. Our concern is the management of the relationship with those who report to you such that you can shape your role more effectively to match your strengths and interests and, in the process, further your own learning and development and the objectives of the organisation for which you work.

Here are some key questions about downward relationships:

➤ Do you understand as much as you might about what motivates each of the people who report to you?

➤ What can you do to help them enhance that motivation?

➤ What does each of them think about you and your style of managing?

➤ Do they have the discretion and responsibility necessary to control their own actions and outputs?

➤ If not, how can you accomplish the required changes?

➤ Does the thought of 'giving away control' in this fashion worry you? If so, you might reflect on why that is and consider what you can do about it.

(ii) Sideways relationships

How do you relate to peers in the organisation or outside, people over whom there is no direct authority? Very often they are crucial to getting things done because they provide raw materials, information, services and they influence your work in some other way. They might be members of other departments, suppliers, customers, unions, and government agencies, co-operative, supportive, friendly in some cases – or, at the other extreme, obstructive, bloody-minded and hostile. Whichever, you have to work with them. And the more you can leave people who report to you to get on with their own tasks, the more time and energy you have to develop relationships with peers and overcome any problems that arise in obtaining their support.

➤ How well do you know those who have the most significant effect on your performance and that of your group? And what can you do to increase that knowledge?

➤ How can you use your knowledge to encourage them to invest more time and effort in providing the necessary service to you and your group?

➤ Do you need to develop certain skills, especially interpersonal, to help you do this?

➤ Are your own attitudes helping or hindering the relationships? In particular, do you co-operate with them willingly when they have a problem you can help solve?

(iii) Upward relationships

Relationships with bosses are critical, as we noted when considering the mirror-image! We depend on them for information and other resources, for co-operation and support. Imagine that your boss has read the questions under 'downward relationships' and is wondering how you can be helped to become more self-motivated and autonomous. He or she might be wary about giving you sufficient discretion to enable this to happen. So what can be done?

➤ How much do you know about your boss's job and his or her feelings about it?
➤ Are there parts you could do and would like to do, especially any that are central to your role and to the performance of your group?
➤ Or can you acquire new skills and knowledge necessary to do parts of the job?
➤ How can you persuade your boss to delegate these aspects and, more generally, to give you sufficient discretion and resources to enable you and your group to become more autonomous?

Make notes of your responses to these three sub-items, especially any important connections between them. Discuss the conclusions with your friend before making a summary of key points to carry forward to Chapter 4.

(E) Handling differences of values

Here you are encouraged to review your own values and how they relate to values that are crucial to understanding the organisation in which you work.

In this section we dig beneath the difficulties encountered in role relationships to explore some of the issues of individual values and how these interact with the values which are widely held within the organisation or its constituent parts. More generally we believe that questions of values and how these are understood and handled are essential to the development of managers and the roles they fulfil.

Difficulties are often caused by diverse values held by those who have key expectations about a manager's role and the behaviour appropriate to that role. These values might concern the organisation, the department or function in which the manager works, the group led by the manager and the tasks they are involved in. For example, we may place a high value on doing a full-day's work and doing it to the best of our ability. But we might place a similar or even higher value on our family's happiness and wish to ensure that the demands of work do not encroach on the attention we give to the family's members. Others in the group, however, might not have an immediate family, or might place a higher priority on career advancement.

So by values we are referring to principles which we hold dear. At their strongest they represent ideals about which we care deeply, sometimes passionately. Values provide certain relatively enduring standards for evaluating and judging proposals, actions and ideas. They help us make decisions. If we say 'that's a good idea', we are probably implying that it meets certain principles which we hold to, more or less consciously.

Value differences and their resolution

Members of a group may also share values about the group's work which can be more important than the questions on which they are divided, especially when dealing with other groups in the organisation. For example, in the computer company, Matrix, in which Neil Compton worked earlier in his career, computer scientists and software engineers placed a higher value on inventing new methods and doing interesting things generally than they did on meeting customer needs; production engineers on the other hand wanted to get something built therefore they valued known rather than new production techniques; meanwhile, salesmen were desperate to meet perceived customer needs and would promise almost anything – even if it didn't yet exist!

Values here were two-edged: they provided a strong bond between those who shared certain functions critical to the organisation's success; but they also served to differentiate one section from another as they competed for resources and other sources of power. Each saw themselves as 'the company', or at least the centre of it. Senior managers had to devote much effort to managing the conflict and allocating resources between them.

This is why an organisation is probably more effective where those senior managers with overall responsibility for its success share certain values which are essential to the overall mission. The shared values help them in their task of integrating the activities of various departments, sub-units and individuals, by resolving differences between them.

Peters and Waterman[4] studied a set of US companies noted for their excellent performance to try to determine the factors that distinguished those organisations from their less successful competitors. A key element seemed to be the values with which collective activities were infused. In many of the excellent companies, leaders had created a distinct set of values which they modelled consistently in their own behaviour and projected in other ways in their day-to-day actions.

In this way leaders communicate values in order to help others interpret events, make decisions and take actions in a consistent way. As Peters and Waterman put it, the excellent companies 'make meanings' for their members. But they acknowledged the darker side of such situations. The excellent companies are marked by such a strong set of values 'that you either buy into their norms or get out. There's no halfway house for most people in the excellent companies... . The companies that make meanings for so many repel others'.[5]

'Buy in – or get out!'

This is just a strong statement of the situations found in most long-standing organisations: however 'excellent' they are it is likely that strong general values operate which may conflict to some extent with the personal values of some individuals within the organisation (see Box 3). That is why it is important for managers' states of mind and general development that they try to be clear about the relationship of their personal values to those generally held in the organisation and especially by the top management group.

Box 3

DIVERGENT VALUES

Until recently Gillian Ramsey was Human Resources Manager for a subsidiary company of a large international enterprise. Early on in her career with them she was arrogant or naïve enough to believe that she could change things, and in certain decentralised activities there was some considerable scope. But as she progressed upwards Gillian found the clash of values and her inability to influence those of the parent organisation's top management more and more frustrating.

She believed in openness with employees, collectively about such things as manpower forecasts, and individually about career potential and other feedback which would help an employee develop. Senior managers in the parent organisation wanted to persuade the world outside of the company's openness as part of a public relations drive but did not see the connection with the inside. Gillian valued collaboration between managers and professionals from different functions and at different levels; for her this was consistent with a technology which seemed to call for interdependence and shared responsibilities. It also squared with the extensive resources devoted to training for effective group working. But in Gillian's view this risked being largely negated by an increasingly vigorous drive to introduce greater competition into salary treatment. Within the system imposed, if anyone's performance for salary purposes was to be improved then someone else's, somewhere, had to go down!

Values are difficult to deal with: it is not always easy to establish what our own values are and just as difficult to sort out the key values of the group or organisation in which we work. Problems are two-fold: values are often not explicit, but are expressed in daily actions or in the artifacts with which people surround themselves; and even when they are explicit, values are rarely freely discussed. This is why Peters and Waterman were surprised at the willingness of the chief executives of their 'excellent companies' to talk about the values which were important to them.

But even if values are rarely expressed openly or are implicit in the organisation's life, clues can be found in the physical surroundings and in the way things are written, for example in company magazines or policy documents. But key values are often expressed in people's daily lives as they act out quite deeply-buried shared assumptions about what is right and wrong. Because the value of 'competition' was just such a taken-for-granted value in her organisation, Gillian Ramsey had so much difficulty in getting her colleagues to discuss its implications when applied very narrowly to salary administration.

(i) Accessing your personal values

So how can you get access to your values and those of the organisation for which you work? To start with, do some work by yourself. Already you may have some clear views on those of your own values which are relevant to organisational life in some direct or indirect way. If not:

Spend some time thinking about the principles which seem to guide you when judging other people's actions or any proposals they might make. Then:

➤ Make notes of these in your workbook. Try to rank the values that you write down in order of importance to you.
➤ Ask some of your friends and close colleagues to reflect on your behaviour and to give feedback on the values you seem to apply in action.

➤ From their responses make a rough listing of values in order of priority as they seem to perceive them. Compare this with your own listing and note any discrepancies which you can attempt to work on and clarify as far as you think necessary.

(ii) ...and organisational values

Now try something similar for the organisation as a whole, the department in which you work, and any small group of which you are a regular participant. Before doing anything else:

➤ Reflect on your own experience, listing in your workbook key events which made you feel very happy or very unhappy and frustrated.

➤ Review what happened — the issues, the behaviour of the various actors — and try to tease out any principles involved.

➤ Concentrate on the emotions you experienced — pleasurable or painful — to help you focus on any clash of values.

➤ Make notes of your findings and then discuss the same questions with colleagues. See if you can corroborate or contradict your initial views.

Don't be surprised if, at this stage, you are confused. It's early days, especially if you are not used to considering questions of this sort. You might find it helpful to talk to some friends from outside the organisation. Their distance may help them 'see the wood among the trees'.

➤ Help your friends by telling them some of the unusual things you noted when you first joined the organisation; what caused you to feel excited or uneasy; and what elements, if any, still give you difficulties. Describe some of the people who are revered — those we might call the 'heroes' or 'champions'. You might comment too on those who are treated as outsiders and, yet, are still tolerated by the organisation — the 'villains' or 'clowns' about the place. If you find it easier, you might like to draw pictures representing situations in the organisation and your feelings about them. For many people images are a very potent way of getting beneath the surface reality.

➤ Encourage your friends to interpret the things you tell them or the images you draw for them and see how far their interpretations support or contradict yours.

➤ Then spend some time privately going over the conversations and updating your initial views on values which seem to be operating in your immediate group, or department, or in the organisation at large. Look for good and bad features.

➤ Finally, refer back to your notes on personal values and compare these with the values which seem to be important collectively. How do you feel about what emerges? Are there large areas of agreement? Are some of the values you hold dear at odds with the collective ones? What implications, if any, might this hold for your future career in the organisation?

Discuss these broader questions with your chosen friend, seeking again to clarify any key points which are more likely to be important for your development. Finalise your notes on this section with a brief forward-looking commentary focusing on those key factors which you can consider in Chapter 4 when beginning to make definite plans to progress your development.

(F) Managerial power

You are asked to examine your own power base and how you use and feel about your power as a manager.

Power is central to organisations. Without some individuals or groups having the power to influence others — to get them to do what they might not have done otherwise — it is not possible to set collective goals, to make plans and achieve those goals, and to take action to implement those plans. Though power is rarely displayed blatantly most members of organisations are aware of its presence and its importance in achieving controlled collective performance.

Power is not limited to those formally appointed as 'managers'; it is open to all sorts of people in various positions throughout an organisation. But managers have several advantages: the positions they occupy, by definition, give them certain potential power generally within a prescribed area of authority; and the placing of those positions in the organisation tends to put managers at key cross-roads between departments, between hierarchical layers, and between the organisation and the world outside. Managers are, in effect, located where the action is — where some of the more crucial events occur and where there is access to information and other resources which are denied, or are less readily accessible, to those not officially called managers. Sources of power, both personal and collective, are described in Box 4:

Box 4

SOURCES OF POWER

Members of organisations have two main sources of power, giving them the potential to influence the behaviour of others inside and outside the organisation. One source is vested in the individual and the position he or she occupies; the other is a collective source of power, derived from membership of groups, sections or departments within the organisation. These two sources are described here.

Power based in the individual stems from one or more of five factors:

- **Authority** delegated to the incumbents of formal positions to make decisions affecting others.
- **Charisma,** or power of personality or character, such that others are willing to be led by the person possessing charisma.
- **Reward power** of those who control the granting of rewards desired by others, such as interesting tasks, pay and promotion.

- **Coercion,** where one person can administer penalties, such as dismissal and withdrawal of friendship, which others would prefer to avoid.
- **Expert** knowledge or skill which others need to achieve their goals.

A group has **collective power** where it is able to:
- Control the supply of essential resources into the organisation.
- Deal with uncertainty facing the organisation by, for example, forecasting, assessing risks and dealing with key external agencies.
- Play a vital role in important organisational decision processes.
- Become a central part of one or more key operations.

But individuals or groups will continue to enjoy the use of that power only as long as the source of their power is irreplaceable by the organisation.

Those with whom we work begin to give us their support more willingly once they feel that, in practice, we use our array of potential power sources to assist the achievement of collective goals without unduly neglecting their important personal interests. As our 'track record' is established, others depend on us more, trust us more and, hence, submit more willingly to our attempts to influence them.

All types of power described in the box can be used in a positive way to further some collective activity to which the individual contributes or, conversely, can be used in a negative way to hinder developments. Such negative power use is generally attributed to those in comparatively low-level positions in organisations who may feel that this is their only access to influence. Against this background:

➤ How do you assess your personal power base in the organisation as compared to your peers, under the five headings in the box?
➤ To what extent, and in what way, do you share in the collective power of a group or section of which you are a member?

➤ How far do you rely on position power to influence those with whom you work?

➤ How far has your career enabled you to build up expertise? Is the field of your expertise growing in importance or on the wane? If on the wane, does this matter to you? And if so, what do you propose to do about it?

➤ How important is it for you that your expertise is recognised? If you feel that the contribution made by your expertise is insufficiently recognised, in what ways would you wish to change things, and how?

➤ How do you use any influence that derives from your membership of a more powerful part of the organisation?

➤ Can you recall situations where you have used negative power, or imagine settings in which you might be prepared to do so? Explore the feelings you had or how you would expect to feel in the future.

➤ Does the use of negative power by others make you angry? Even if their behaviour is only a sign of how little positive power they feel able to bring to bear?

Once you have made notes under each of these headings test out some of your preliminary findings with close colleagues, revise the commentary as necessary and then discuss it with your friend. Before moving on, prepare a carry-forward summary for use at the overall planning stage.

(G) Political awareness and skills

In this last section we explore how you behave in the organisation as a political arena, with a view to improving your awareness and political skills without compromising any of your deeply held beliefs and values.

The use of power in practice rarely goes unchallenged. Organisations are made up of different individuals and formal and informal groups with varied and sometimes conflicting interests. Coalitions are formed between individuals and between groups with compatible interests so as to increase their collective power to achieve shared goals.

Individual differences

Where do different organisational interests come from? To start with, each individual in an organisation has a unique blend of interests. Members pursue their interests with more or less energy and commitment. Some of these interests may relate quite directly to the role performed and the power, prestige, or other more tangible rewards to which the role gives access. People may also have career aspirations which stimulate them to seek out situations where talents can be demonstrated and recognised. The difficulty is to obtain sufficient visibility without 'getting up the nose' of bosses and others who might help a career along, including peers and subordinates! Other personal interests are imported into the organisation, perhaps linked to membership of a certain profession, trade union or other external movement.

Coalitions

From this personal perspective it is easy to move to a view of an organisation as a set of coalitions of people with common interests. Certain aspects of organisations encourage coalitions. Hierarchical, functional, and other formal divisions fragment the organisation's members into separate interest groups which have different, if overlapping, goals and activities. While there may be some general level of support for overall values and goals, such fragmentation of the organisational structure often results in conflict over specific objectives and programmes, further fuelled by the differing interests of individuals. Less powerful actors may seek coalitions to help protect their positions; those with more influence may attempt to consolidate power through coalition, or by advancing the interests of others who, in return, can be expected to support them later. Social activities — golf, dinners, theatre, etc — provide private relaxed settings for coalition building.

Hence organisational life encourages a wide variety of political activity in that it encompasses systems of simultaneous competition and collaboration. In pursuit of a common goal people must vie with each other for limited resources, status, and career advancement. Competition may be between different levels in the hierarchy, eg as workers try to outwit management in the setting and control of standards of work. Specialised units and individuals at the same level also compete – production vs marketing, line vs staff.

In such contexts it is not surprising that some people are described as 'political animals'. But what does this mean? That they are sensitive to the informal norms and formal rules that operate in any situation and know how to make those rules and norms work for them? And that they know who to lobby and how to recruit them to their point of view? Or does the description 'political' imply dishonesty? Or at least game playing without regard to the interests and feelings of other participants?

In this arena where personal and collective interests are worked out through political processes, you might like to examine your own position by responding to questions and prompts under the headings of political awareness, visibility, autonomy, and relevance.

(i) Political awareness

This dimension takes account of how far you can 'read' the organisation and the behaviour of the key people within it and use the formal and informal structures and processes to fulfil your role – and with it your obligations to the organisation – and to advance your personal interests.

➤ Do you understand the organisation's mission and how your departmental objectives relate to it?
➤ Do you know how major decisions are made, formally and informally, which affect you and your group?
➤ Do you understand where the key locations of power are in the organisation and on what that power is based?
➤ How does your power and the use you make of it relate to those key power sources?
➤ Are you tuned in to the managerial grape vine?

(ii) Visibility[6]

This dimension is about the extent to which you and your work are known within the organisation.

➤ Who knows about, or could be told about, your ambitions and career aspirations?

➤ In what ways — through formal reviews, informal conversations, reports, etc — are what you do and the way that you do it communicated beyond your immediate workgroup?

➤ How can you build bridges into the organisation through influential people in your department, through job activities which bring you into contact with people outside the department, and through participation in cross-organisation committees, task forces, etc?

➤ How do you, or could you, benefit from participation in groups and professional organisations external to the organisation?

(iii) Autonomy[6]

This harks back to the section on relationships where we questioned ways in which you could increase the autonomy of your group in relation to you, and of yourself in reflection to your boss.

➤ How much discretion do you, or could you, have to make decisions without reference to others?

➤ What scope do you, or could you, have to take initiatives and, hence, to show your creativity?

➤ How could you get involved in new projects or activities which provide scope to demonstrate your capabilities?

(iv) Relevance[6]

Finally, we look at the dimension of relevance which is concerned with the significance of your role to crucial and urgent organisational issues.

➤ Could you list three crucial and urgent issues? And in relation to these issues:

➤ How could your role be shaped to play a more central part?

➤ What skills do you have, or could you acquire, which are most relevant?

That is the last of the perspectives of this Chapter. At this stage we suggest you do two things before moving on. First, discuss your commentary on the points covered under managerial politics with your chosen friend and modify as necessary before making a carry-forward summary of important issues for you and your development.

Second, read through all of the summaries carried forward from the seven perspectives and make any connections. Look for similarities, providing evidence, say, of a certain type of preference or style which you can acknowledge and develop. Or tease out the contradictions which, again, you might attempt to resolve or learn to live with. Don't be too hard on yourself: take full credit for the good parts (and we hope your friend helps you with this); and try not to exaggerate the 'warts': we all have them. And since, in the next and later stages, you will have time and energy to address only a few issues, try to prioritise the factors which emerge in terms of their importance for your development: key strengths to build on, and key shortcomings (if any!) to work on positively and optimistically, but not to mope over!

Notes

1. Nicholson, N and West, M A (1988) *Managerial Job Change: Men and Women in Transition*, Cambridge University Press.
2. Mintzberg, H (1973) *The Nature of Managerial Work*, New York: Harper & Row.
3. Kotter, J P (1982) 'What effective general managers actually do' *Harvard Business Review*, Nov/Dec.
4. Peters, T J and Waterman, R H (1982) *In Search of Excellence*, London: Harper & Row.
5. Peters and Waterman, p 77.

6. The three factors of visibility, autonomy and relevance used here are taken from a questionnaire ('Four factors shaping power and influence') by Goodmeasure, of Cambridge, Massachusetts, which is reproduced in Morgan, G (1989) *Creative Organization Theory: A Resource Book*, California: Sage.

Chapter 3
Personal Resources in Managing and Learning From Change

Introduction

For the most part in Chapter 2 we stressed managerial behaviour – the actions that managers take in certain situations and the skills required to act effectively. Now we turn to look inward at personal resources which underpin that behaviour. We focus on certain aspects of personality and preferred styles of being and acting which distinguish one person from another. A few were dealt with directly in the previous chapter, such as personal values, attitudes toward peers, feelings about power and control, and sensitivity to situations. Others were alluded to, as when we considered self-image related to preferred managerial roles. In this chapter we look at some of these and other aspects of personal resources in greater detail.

We do not attempt to deal with all possible resources. Instead we concentrate on those which are likely to be most useful in situations of change and ambiguity. Our main concern is with all that adds to flexibility, and enhances adaptation and learning.

Today more than ever managers are subject to a flow of change prompted by events external to the particular organisations for which they work. They are expected to anticipate and respond to events in a way which maintains the organisation's potential for transformation. Conversely, managers are frequently required, or choose for themselves, to create new and improved ways of doing things, 'to be ahead of the competition'. The continual flux which results – part reactive, part self-induced – is a key theme emerging from the Managerial Survey. And, as already noted, the managers responding to the survey who were most active in shaping their roles also thought that the experience had advanced their personal development in some significant way. Hence our decision to stress change, innovation and learning in this chapter.

Many researchers, practitioners and theorists have attempted to describe the sorts of personal resources which are important for effective managers. From their studies and writings we have abstracted a variety of factors which seem to be crucial to our dual theme of managing change effectively and of furthering personal development in the process. More detail about our sources can be found in the various endnotes and in detailed comments in the last section of Chapter 5.

The resulting word-portrait of the innovative and learning manager is drawn under these headings:

(A) *Purpose and Proactivity* (pp. 67–8) – some general sense of purpose that extends beyond the narrow managerial role and the relationship of such purposefulness to a proactive style of managing.

(B) *Feelings and their Control* (pp. 69–70) – the relationship between emotions and feelings on the one hand and motivation on the other, noting how crucial it seems to be that feelings are acknowledged and harnessed in the interests of effective action.

(C) *Creative Style* (pp. 70–78) – five dimensions of creative style are considered: flexible perceptions; supple thinking; being relaxed with complexity; playing it cool when the pressure is on to close things down; and making judgements on the basis of incomplete data.

(D) *Learning Habits* (pp. 78–85) – finally, the notion of a learning loop, moving from experience in action, to abstract ideas and theories, to practical proposals for further action. We pay particular attention to handling feedback, effective listening, and increasing self-knowledge through introspection.

What do we propose to use this portrait for? One thing is clear: it is not intended to be an 'ideal type' toward which every manager should strive. However flexible our personalities and styles are, it would be destructive to try to become *supermanagers*. They do not exist and people created on these lines would be insufferable!

Much more useful than the overall portrait are the elements

of which it is composed. By considering yourself along each of the dimensions represented you will, most importantly, enhance your self-knowledge. As we argue in the text this is central to self-management and personal development. One possible outcome is that you opt to make the best of exactly who you are, playing from your strengths quite deliberately.

On the other hand, you may decide to try to change certain aspects of yourself and the personal resources you can command – for example, by developing certain dimensions of your creative style or by strengthening aspects of your learning style. Looking ahead, we point out in Chapter 5 some of the ways in which you might follow up these sorts of decisions.

Improved self-knowledge also gives you another option: to change the context in which you work as a manager, or even to decide to stop being a manager and do something else. As we shall see in Chapter 4, this was the decision taken by Gillian Ramsey whose value dilemma was mentioned above. For people who are considering major transitions we deal with some of the key issues in Chapter 5.

As for the process you might follow through this chapter, we suggest that, if you have started a workbook, you continue to use it. We recommend that you do not try to develop firm proposals at an early stage of working through any particular section. More important is the building up of your own portrait and, perhaps, starting to highlight those parts, if any, on which you might concentrate attention.

As before, talk through your ideas with a friend, to help you fill in the picture that emerges. We will continue through this chapter to prompt you about note-taking and exploring your ideas and feelings in discussion.

(A) Purpose and proactivity

In this first section we examine two aspects of the portrait: First, the importance of some general sense of purpose that extends beyond the narrow field of managerial role and, second, a proactive style within which assertiveness is seen as natural.

Managers who deal effectively with change and challenge seem to have a strong sense of purpose, not concerned solely with personal goals but with broader issues within the community. They might, for example, play a role in an industry or professional association; sit on the magistrates' bench; devote considerable time to some charity to which, perhaps, they are drawn by family circumstances. Purpose provides a sense of direction for people's actions, supplying an important part of motivation. When we are purposeful we are also more likely to have the confidence to be proactive — creating or controlling situations by taking initiatives. Successful managers appear to be more proactive, responding to events which relate to their sense of purpose as if navigating by some very personal, wide-ranging and longer-term set of goals. For them it is natural to be assertive, to advance arguments in pursuit of their general purposes or more personal interests and needs.[1]

Notions of purpose also blend in with the concept of 'need for growth' which was used to assess people's level of motivation in the Managerial Survey. People with a high need for growth tend to want challenging work; a job where they can be creative in doing things their own way; to acquire knowledge and skills; and to contribute to society.

➤ How do you respond to the notion of purposefulness? Does it square with how you see, or would want to see, yourself?

➤ In what sort of situations do you tend to be more proactive? And less so? Can you account for the reason for your willingness to take the initiative in certain contexts and not others?

➤ How easy do you find it to assert yourself, insisting that your purposes and interests be taken into account? Does this vary according to context?

Talk these issues over with your friend and make brief notes to carry forward.

(B) Emotions, feelings, and their control

Here we explore how far you have access to your emotions and feelings and are able to express and direct them in a positive way.

If the goals we claim to pursue and the values that those goals imply do matter to us then it is likely we will have strong feelings about them. In effect, emotions and feelings fuel our actions, providing motivational energy which enables us to achieve the goals we have set ourselves. But this relationship between emotions and goals works consistently only if we are aware of our feelings and are prepared to acknowledge them and their importance for us. Then we are less likely to be at the whim of our emotions but, instead, are able to control them in pursuit of our goals.

Control implies that we can regulate and direct the flow of emotional energy. We can better ensure that its force is appropriate to the events which confront us, that it is stable over a sufficient period of time, and that we have access to a deep enough source of energy. When people talk about persistence and stability these are the dimensions of motivation and personality which are implied.

Effective control of emotions is different from suppression. Control means we acknowledge our emotions but wish them to be our servants, not our masters. Once this sort of self-accepting control is achieved we have emotional resilience; coping with stressful events — which are the lot of many managers — is easier. As was found in the Managerial Survey, people often seem to learn substantially in the transition from an uncomfortable, stressful state to a more comfortable one. Anxiety gives way, perhaps slowly, to confidence, and confusion is translated into understanding.

So we don't have to be 'thick-skinned' and insensitive to weather difficult situations. Instead, by knowing our feelings and relating them to our goals in a controlled way, we are more likely to know when to push on and when to yield. That is the nature of resilience.

➤ How do you think you handle stressful situations? By suppressing your emotions? Or by acknowledging them and allowing them to work for you?

➤ Think of a recent event which made you anxious because you were uncertain what was going to happen next. What sort of emotions and feelings did you experience? How did you deal with them?

➤ Who, if anyone, do you usually talk over such incidents with? How do they perceive your state of emotional control?

Again, make brief notes of your responses to these items. Then discuss them with your friend in order to focus on key aspects to carry forward without necessarily coming to hard and fast conclusions at this stage.

(C) Creative style

Now we move on to look at five aspects of creative style: flexible perceptions; supple thinking; dealing with complexity; keeping things open; and making judgements. The intention is that we become more potent as managers by appreciating and developing the creative side of ourselves and seeking out opportunities for its expression in our various roles.

When we say that some action or behaviour is creative we tend to mean that it has resulted in a unique response or object, which is useful and often gives a pleasant feeling of surprise. Unfortunately the word is most frequently used to describe the behaviour and accomplishments of people in such fields as art, literature, science, and drama. As for the poor old manager or politician, and all others whose raw material is social relationships, their achievements are all too rarely described as creative. And yet they are often confronted with making decisions that are novel, relatively unstructured and of considerable consequence for many others. According to Herbert Simon, who won the Nobel prize for his research on decision-making, such decisions call for considerable judgement, intuition, and creativity.[2]

Creativity is not just the province of the few. We are not talking about 'genius', the relatively rare possession of a very high level of creative ability, but about the capability which most people have to produce good and distinctive solutions to unusual problems, often by bringing existing ideas together in a new form. From this standpoint most people have some potential to be creative.

Certainly those in the Managerial Survey who saw themselves as creative were also more likely to report how they shaped their managerial roles. They spoke of such innovations as 'the implementation of a large software package', 'the creation of a new computer centre', 'a new organisation for materials management', 'the development of a completely new range of merchandise', and 'researching and developing a new short course'.[3] For many people these sorts of challenges will be more or less commonplace, just part of being a manager in a changing situation. And that's exactly our point: creativity is more common than you perhaps think. What you need to do is to recognise and honour it more often and, hence, to see yourself as potentially creative.

So what sorts of skills and attributes seem to be called into play in creative activity? As you might guess there are as many answers as there are commentators on this fascinating subject but we limit ourselves to five broad headings:

(i)   Flexible perceptions
(ii) Supple thinking
(iii) Being relaxed with complexity
(iv) Playing it cool
(v)   Judgement-making

Since repeated advice to make notes and talk to your friend can interfere with the flow, we will prompt you only at the end of the five sub-items. But we suggest that you make draft notes as you go through the items, leaving scope to make vital connections between them at the end as a basis for carrying forward a summary into Chapter 4.

(i) Flexibility in perception

Perception is about understanding what's going on. When we are confronted by an unusual event or situation we need to 'size it up' or to interpret what's happening — to make a judgement of the 'reality out there'. Is this fall in sales a seasonal thing or a result of a competitor's new product? What is the significance of new government policies for our school, or business, or hospital?

A key element in that reality judgement is our sensitivity to what is going on. How tuned in are we to what is happening around us? Are we open to information of all sorts — the 'hard stuff' of facts and opinions and the 'softer impressions' of our own and other people's feelings? Do we begin to appreciate the influence of competitors' new products earlier than others do? Are we alert to what government departments are planning?

Once our antennae are twitching, what sense do we make of the information available to us? Being creative often involves seeing or interpreting 'facts' differently from the way others appreciate them. New information is sifted quickly for its importance; the whole situation is summed up without getting bogged down in the detail of its component parts.

Flexibility in the way we perceive and interpret events depends on being able to rearrange items of information, see them in different settings, envisage unusual uses for things, and relate them in novel ways. But in judging the reality out there we are guided by our interests, values, attitudes and all of life's baggage. To survive at all we need to label things that occur regularly, so that we can understand what's going on — helping us to answer questions like: 'Is this in my interest? Do I value that sort of outcome? How do I generally feel about this type of information?' Hence one of the paradoxes of creativity: we have to label events and things to cope with everyday life but need to retain the facility to ignore labels or change the way we label things when faced with puzzling situations. In this way we are able to take in 'unwelcome' aspects and to create relationships between items normally labelled as quite different from each other.

➤ How do you try to ensure that you are aware of things going on that are likely to affect you?

➤ Do you know how people are feeling and how they are likely to behave in any situation?

➤ What do you find when you compare the sorts of situation and events, if any, which you find difficult to read with those which you find easy?

➤ What does this tell you about the labels you use to categorise information? And what part do the key values identified earlier play here in that labelling?

(ii) Supple thinking

Another paradox: a great difficulty in trying to be creative can be our expertise, for example, as a manager, a teacher, an engineer. Often we draw on that expertise to understand the problem that confronts us in our special field. But once we appreciate that the problem is novel we might need to break out of the thinking straitjacket which expertise can so easily impose. So we need to decide whether the problem is of the sort we can solve almost by programme, bringing to bear an explicit or even a taken-for-granted procedure for arriving at a solution. Then there will generally be little difficulty; we will almost certainly 'hit the jackpot'.

But if it's not the type of problem that responds to recipes then we need a more flexible approach. In a job where many unusual events come along we may already have been shown, or developed ourselves, some strategies for resolving the problems they bring. This could involve ways of arraying and analysing data, or the use of implicit theories (eg about the way people behave, or about the relationship of events in the product market, or about the way civil servants operate), or by reference to previous problems of broadly the same sort.

Even at this higher level of thinking you are likely to encounter a problem from time to time that resists your tested strategies. At this stage the supple thinkers can go back to first principles, breaking out of their preferred approach to find some other unsuspected keys. It's a case of being willing and able to move off in new directions without too much heart-searching and difficulty.

And if your managerial job is as fragmented as those studied by Henry Mintzberg and other researchers (see Chapter 2), then it is likely that this particular problem will not be the only one you are dealing with at the moment. Then, a further test of your suppleness is whether you can switch rapidly and easily from one problem to another.

So, how supple are you when dealing with problems?

➤ Can you distinguish easily between programmed and more ambiguous situations?

➤ Do you find it unsettling to face unusual problems which don't yield easily to your normal approaches to problem-solving?

➤ Can you switch easily from one problem to another? Or would you prefer to concentrate on one until it is solved?

(iii) Being relaxed with complexity

Creativity is especially necessary when we face complex problems, with many angles and contradictory aspects that make varied and confusing demands on us and our skills. Those who perform more creatively than others seem to appreciate working in such situations and have a facility for dealing with complexity. They can think of several things at once, relating different ideas to each other, and often have memories which allow them to code, retain, and recall large amounts of detailed information. Hence they can access quite easily any relevant information built up from previous experience and can retrieve from memory facts about the current problem which have emerged over a period of time.

➤ Do you relish complex situations or do they make you feel very anxious?

➤ However you feel about them, how do you perform when confronted with complex problems? Do your peers see you as having some special skills?

➤ What part do you play in a group of people tackling a complex problem?

(iv) Playing it cool

What do we mean by 'playing it cool'? Well, we have looked at the research evidence and it seems that creativity is frequently associated with the nerve to keep things open, to avoid being stampeded into a decision before you need finally to close down the options. 'But', you might well say, 'doesn't management equal action, getting on with things?' Yes and no. In fact the jibe the Japanese often make at the expense of Western managers, especially Americans, goes something like this:

> 'Yes, you are good at making quick decisions, but look at the mess you make when trying to implement them.'

The Japanese have a reputation for going one step at a time, not knowing exactly what the next step will be but always keeping their eye on a clear goal. So given their track-record of innovation it might be worth adopting the cooler approach they imply.

First, when faced with a very complex and uncertain situation it seems sensible to avoid over-detailed plans for resolving it. If we don't do this, there is a risk of foreclosing on alternative ways of interpreting the situation in the first place and of solving problems identified. While evidence of the value of keeping things open arose initially from research into creative artists, it has been supported in studies of negotiating, a key management skill.[4]

According to the researchers, the successful negotiators spent no less time planning their negotiating strategy than their less effective colleagues but they considered a broader range of options, set their objectives within wider limits, and shied away from the planned sequence for the negotiation which tied issues together restrictively. Such behaviour requires a certain degree of 'cool' in the run up to the first negotiating meeting, especially if the negotiator's bosses want to know exactly what is proposed. Such pressure, and its attendant anxiety, can so easily result in more detailed plans than can possibly work in practice. Though they may be 'pie in the sky' they can provide a veneer of certainty and reassurance. So creativity in such situations may require the ability to withstand a lot of tension and pressure in order to keep options open.

The spin-off is that ideas are more easily generated. In the bargaining context negotiators can explore ideas for resolving common difficulties and extending the scope for mutual benefits before closing down the options and fighting hard over the share-out. 'Brainstorming', a widely used technique for generating ideas, also depends for its effectiveness on keeping options open and suspending judgement. It is assumed that people will offer up ideas much more willingly and fluently if others agree not to rush to evaluate them.

So, how cool are you?

➤ Do you need detailed plans when confronted with complex and uncertain situations? Or can you live with a sketchier, more flexible framework?

➤ Do you feel the tensions mounting as the situation develops and still no solution is forthcoming?

➤ How do you behave then? What strategies do you have for coping?

➤ How do you rate your skill in fending off the pressure of a boss to develop more detailed plans than you think desirable?

Cool, man, cool!

(v) Judgement making

But in the end we have to make a decision, reach some judgement about the various issues involved. And unless we have been very lucky, areas of ambiguity will remain. Many managerial problems hinge on assumptions about the future – markets, products, technology, the political persuasion of the next government, and so on – so certainty is beyond our grasp. We might not even have the best information we would like about aspects of the current situation – because we can't see, for example, what a competitor is up to, or what is happening inside the core of a closed-down reactor, or how many employees are in the union. Often it is too expensive to get all the data we would ideally like.

So we might have to make the best use of the partial information, infer bits which we don't know from those we do and be prepared to rely on our experience and intuition. On the line is our ability to weigh the pros and cons which emerge despite any shortage of facts. However anxious we are, this is the time when feelings come into play as well as rational, logical thought; values as well as data.

And hanging over us as we close things down and move towards a decision is the next paradox of creativity: will the decision be a good one? Just a short while ago we were probably thinking 'why the hell don't we get on with this?', but as pressures mount to make up our mind we tend to procrastinate. This is the factor that leads to decisions being deferred while we just 'get a few more facts'.

Reflect on your approach to making judgements:

➤ How do you feel about having to make decisions in situations where considerable uncertainty remains?

➤ Do you believe in something called 'intuition' where you rely on data that can't be specified?

➤ Are you aware of having used intuition? And if so, how good were the decisions made?

You might care to get feedback from colleagues on this last point.

We have completed our review of the five, interrelated facets of creative style. By now you have probably come to the conclusion we reached when preparing this text, that no one person is likely to possess all of these attributes to a high degree. And since organisational decision-making in conditions of uncertainty generally calls for team-work involving managers and other professionals, this need not be a great disadvantage. In fact, if properly co-ordinated, a team of people bringing complementary perspectives and styles is probably an aid to creativity.

So your aim in note-taking and discussions with your friend at this stage might be to picture your particular style of creativity. In future you can then be better prepared to take a lead in situations which call for your strengths, and to support colleagues in other contexts to which your profile is less well matched. And, as we shall see in Chapter 5, there are ways of modifying creative style through courses of training.

(D) Learning habits

In this final section on personal resources we ask you to examine your own preferred style of learning as between experience in action, reflection in order to develop abstract ideas and theories, and the development of practical proposals for action. Then we concentrate on three aspects of your learning habits: handling feedback, effective listening, and acquiring self-knowledge.

There is evidence that managers who have the reputation for being wise and of sound judgement are more open to learning from new experiences. In particular they seem to have these key skills and qualities:

- They learn from mistakes.
- They are prepared for critical negative feedback.
- They listen and reflect.
- They have self-knowledge.

These skills probably account in part for why some people appear to be more independent than others in learning situations. Successful managers tend not to rely heavily on teachers and experts but are more prepared than others to make their own minds up about the rightness of things learned.[5] Their style in this seems to be well described by the learning loop shown in Figure 2.

Out of practical experience managers derive feedback direct from the outcome itself (how successful was the action? did the implied theories work in practice? etc), and from others who took part, and from any more detached observers. Then they reflect on that feedback and are able to develop abstract ideas or theories to explain what happened. Notions such as this may not be explicit, or capable of conscious expression, but eventually emerge in action. Not only are successful managers able to reflect and think abstractly but they can relate the ideas or budding theories into real-life situations and, hence, develop practical proposals. Finally, they are then able to move into the action phase and find opportunities to implement the proposals and, hence, test out the validity of any underlying ideas.

Think of yourself within that learning loop:

➤ In what situations, if any, do you rely on experts?
➤ How easily do you relate theory and practice? And does this include trying out your own pet ideas in practice?
➤ Do you enjoy reflection or are you more of an action person?

Certain aspects of the learning loop have been dealt with earlier in this section of the book: thinking processes in the last section on creative style, and the use of practice and experience in Chapter 2. So now we propose to concentrate on the processes of feedback and reflection, including listening skills and self-knowledge through introspection.

As with creativity, individuals have different preferred styles of learning. For example, some like to read up the theory before acting. Others get into action early and reflect on their experience. But most people are able to operate in all phases of the cycle when the situation requires. Again, it is a question of preferences and strengths, rather than one or the other.

(i) Handling feedback

Feedback comes directly from outcomes of events we are involved in — did we achieve our goals? If not, by how far did we miss them? What went right and wrong? This is the sort of information on which 'debriefings' concentrate, focused on results.

Another sort of feedback, related but of a different quality, is about the processes involved in achieving results and how

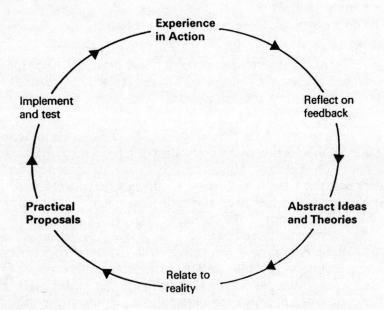

Figure 2 *The learning loop*

those processes were experienced. As a manager we get information of this sort from a variety of sources: people who work for us, bosses, peers, friends and casual observers. It is often expressed in feelings: 'euphoria' in the members of a team who really got their act together; 'anger' on the part of someone who felt badly treated; the 'bewilderment' of a person confronted with contradictory messages and behaviour.

Often feedback is hard to take: on the one hand we might be bruised by criticism aimed at us for not achieving results or for the way we behaved towards colleagues; or embarrassed by praise, not able to take it because of our own poor self-image. But if we are to learn from experience we have to be able to take the potential rough and smooth of feedback and to benefit from both.

Dilemmas of handling feedback are nicely captured by Mike Pedler and Tom Boydell in Figure 3 taken from their book *Managing Yourself*. It is part of their argument that individuals are hardly likely to be able to manage tasks and people if they cannot manage themselves. For Pedler and Boydell, handling and learning from feedback is a key part of development.

In Chapter 2 we made a brief reference to 'game-playing' as part of the political behaviour. People are more likely to indulge in this when they find it difficult to respond to feedback in other than a 'non-constructive, regressive manner' (see Figure 3). Faced with unpalatable feedback, game-playing helps them to maintain false images ('I am bad, unworthy of praise' or 'I am brilliant; when is the rest of the world going to catch on?') and to avoid feelings that contradict those images. In fact, game-playing is about manipulating people so that they give us only feedback that confirms our self-image. Post mortems and reviews of decisions can soon degenerate in this way, especially in high-risk situations. On the other hand game-playing is less likely when trust in the group is high and when, as individuals, we are able to be more honest with ourselves and to admit the possibility of improvement.

➡ How do you relate to the notion of feedback summed up in Figure 3?

➤ Do you ever catch yourself playing games in the way described? In what sort of situations does this happen? Is there anything you want to do about it?

Make notes on these points and talk them over with your friend before moving on.

(ii) Effective listening

You may know the expression 'they listen but don't hear', often used about someone who is thought to be politically unaware. This is probably because that person concentrates on the rational level – of words, abstract ideas and thoughts – but fails to pick up the more subtle messages about emotions and feelings and about purpose and intentions. If you can persuade three others to join in you might like to test out your skill in getting behind the words by doing the simple exercise described in Box 5.[7]

Box 5

LISTENING SKILLS

The purpose of this exercise is to help you to listen on three levels:

(a) listening at a 'head' level to thoughts and words;
(b) listening at a 'heart' level to feelings and emotions;
(c) listening at a 'will' level to real intentions.

Ideally this exercise should be done in a group of four people. One person should volunteer to be the 'talker'. This person should tell a short, real story about an issue that is as yet unresolved. It can be connected to home or work and should be about five minutes long. Each of the three 'listeners' elects to listen on *one* level only:

(a) 'Thinking', that is, listen to the words and the *thoughts* behind the words. How the story is told – fast, slow, in a clear logical progression or mixed, jumbled and circular. Are the words descriptive or factual, etc.
(b) 'Feeling', that is, listen to the *feeling* behind the words. How is that person feeling now, in this room telling the story, how did they feel about what was happening in different parts of their story?

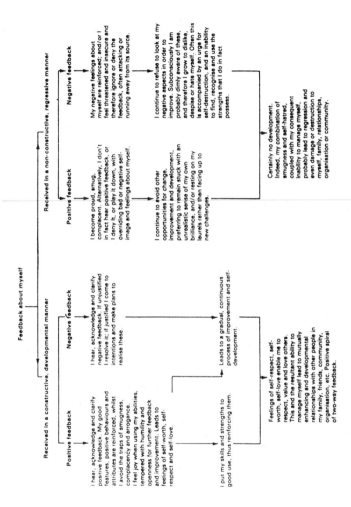

Figure 3 *Handling and learning from feedback*

Source: Pedler, M and Boydell, T (1985) *Managing Yourself*, London: Fontana Paperbacks.

(c) 'Willing', that is, listen to the real *will* and intention which comes through the words. What is their real intention or which way are they inclining in this unresolved issue?

At the end of the story each of the listeners feedback about two minutes of what they have heard. In their descriptions they should stay within the level of their listening. At the end of each feedback the talker should confirm whether or not they were accurately received.

This process is to be repeated until each person in the quartet has experienced all the roles. Then discuss this with a view to seeing any surprises and discovering lessons for the future in how you will try to listen and understand.

Make notes of the outcome and discuss with your friend.

(iii) *Acquiring self-knowledge through introspection*

Learning and personal development are unlikely to take place if we have little self-knowledge. Already this need has cropped up a number of times, most notably in the discussion of emotions and feelings in Section B above. Without an understanding of our own purpose, values, attributes, fears and hopes, we are unlikely to be able to explain and control our behaviour and its influence on the outcomes of important events in which we are involved. As managers we are a key dynamic element in the unfolding events. Unlike scientists or technicians, or even artists, the material of our creativity is not all 'out there', separate from us. Like them we are responsible for the creative process but are also part of it; the material on which we have to work our art or craft as a manager includes us. And until we can begin to unravel at a conscious or intuitive level the effects we are having, then our interpretations of events and our ability to influence the interpretations and actions of those around us are likely to be unnecessarily restricted.

To lift these restrictions it is important to be able to reflect, to take time to look inward, to be introspective – even if what we see is not always to our liking! How do we relate to this dimension?

➤ Are you aware of situations where self-knowledge of purpose, values, feelings, etc, affected your behaviour?

➤ Has your level of self-awareness been developed through special efforts at introspection?

➤ How far have you been helped to reflect and introspect by the questions in this whole section?

As at the end of the last chapter, if you are still following the review process through, do the following things – first, make brief notes of this last item and discuss them with your friend in order to clarify your ideas on this aspect of yourself. Then gather together all of the notes carried forward from this chapter on purpose and proactivity, feelings and their control, creative style and learning habits. Look for connections between them that seem to be important in building up a coherent 'self-portrait' on the various dimensions. And focus on common themes that strike you as the most significant when you consider yourself in this overall frame. Finally, make brief summary notes of your whole personal resources review to carry forward to the next stage introduced in Chapter 4.

Notes

1. See Pedler, M, Burgoyne, J and Boydell, T (1986) *A Manager's Guide to Self-development*, Maidenhead: McGraw-Hill.
2. Herbert Simon makes a distinction between 'programmable and non-programmable decisions (which require intuition and creativity)' in a paper published in a collection of readings, Pugh, D (Ed.) (1984) *Organisation Theory*, Harmondsworth: Penguin.
3. Reported by Nicholson, N and West, M A (1988) *Managerial Job Change: Men and Women in Transition*, Cambridge.
4. This comes from a very interesting piece of research into the real-life behaviour of negotiators: Rackham, N and Carlisle, J (1978) 'The effective negotiator' in *The Journal of European Industrial Training*, 2(6) and (7).
5. See Pedler, Burgoyne and Boydell (1986) mentioned in note 1 above.
6. The notion of a learning loop is similar to David Kolb's learning cycle introduced in the 1970s and developed specifically for use

in management development by Peter Honey and Alan Mumford in *The Manual of Learning Styles* (1986). They argue that people tend to prefer one or more of four learning styles — 'activist', 'reflector', 'theorist' and 'pragmatist' — depending on the stage in the learning cycle where they learn best. An eighty item self-report questionnaire is included as part of the manual for readers to determine their own preferred style. They are then encouraged to consider how they can 'play from their strength', by capitalising on their preferred style, or strive to become an 'all-round learner' by overcoming existing weaknesses.

7. This is an extract from page 105 of the book by Jane Skinner and Rennie Fritchie (1988) *Working Choices: A Life-planning Guide for Women Today*, London: Dent.

Chapter 4
Personal Planning Within a
Life-Career Frame

In this chapter we invite you to integrate any ideas and wishes about your job as a manager which were stimulated by the previous chapters into a broader frame of life and career, and to begin to look forward to possible futures. The twin aims are to help you:

(i) To make decisions about your present job and future career (including doing nothing different!)
(ii) To try to ensure that those decisions fit well with, and preferably enrich, other aspects of your life, especially close relationships with family and others.

In working toward those aims we make several connected assumptions:

- Work and career cannot be appreciated and planned for independently of the rest of a person's life: key events in any part of his or her life are likely to affect other parts.
- An individual's personal life has continuity and yet there is scope to develop by changing what is done and the way it is done.
- The cumulative effect of people changing what they do and how they do it is to change themselves: how they think and feel about themselves, and how others perceive and respond to them.
- A career is not a path ready laid out for you to follow; it only becomes real with hindsight. No firm and detailed predictions can be made about future steps. The best you can do is to have some sense of direction; a balance between persistence and flexibility — so that you know when to press on despite difficulties and when to change course; and a short-range plan of some specific things you intend to change.

Life's levels, arenas and timescale

Lives are lived at different levels and in multiple arenas, as illustrated in Figure 4. The 'public person' engaging in managerial and other roles reveals a personality – made up of a regular pattern of attitudes, motivations and behaviours – that is recognised by others and the individual. Deeper down is the level of the 'private self' where perceptions, thoughts, feelings and emotions are experienced by the individual alone; this level provides the foundation for the personal resources which people bring to bear in their public lives.

Looking outward, lives are acted out in many arenas. Managers have lives in the organisation for which they work; in the broader community, and among family and friends. Any individual's life, and the total person they have become, is experienced through the overlap of the various roles and the relationships that make up those roles.

Apart from life's levels and arenas, there is a third dimension: time. Through life's course and the career that forms part of it, our capabilities and roles change in each of the arenas. There is a dynamic link between achievements in the various roles which we act out and our capabilities to fulfil those and novel roles. We learn and develop through our experience so that, even as the biological base of our intellectual and physical capacities begins to erode with age, we have the potential to make good use of that which remains in our continuing contributions to the varying levels and arenas of our life.

At this stage in our review we suggest that you now attempt to integrate into this broader life framework the pen-portrait of yourself as a manager which you have been drawing so far. In particular we ask you to focus on key themes which may have been a recurring feature of your life so far and on the links between your life as a manager and your life in other key arenas. Our aim in doing this is to ensure as far as possible that any plans you make arising from this personal review carry forward key life themes and are complementary with your life in other roles and arenas.

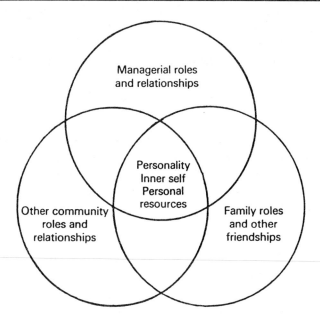

Figure 4 *Levels and arenas of life activities*

Picturing the past

We start by looking into the past again but this time job and career are placed into a total picture showing how you reacted to and felt about key incidents and episodes in your life. We suggest you prepare that picture in the following steps, discussing each with your friend whenever you feel that will help you to resolve issues and make progress.

(i) Focus on incidents

Think back over your life, starting at either end, and write down the most important things that happened, which you did or which were done to you, that had some significant outcomes both practical and emotional. Include the changes of organisation which you were asked to list as part of the review of managerial experience in Chapter 2.

It's probably best to take plenty of time over this step; ponder for a few days if needs be, gradually building up a list, changing it as necessary to reflect only the most significant incidents.

(ii) Plot a life-line

Once you are satisfied with the list, plot the incidents with comments on a life-career chart of jobs of the sort shown for Neil Compton in Figure 5. Once you have marked in the incidents draw a curve as Neil has done to represent your feelings, rising upwards when things went well and you felt good, sinking right down when you felt particularly bad. Take care to draw out any interplay between experiences in your life's different arenas and the roles you play in each. An example is the family tensions caused by Neil's extensive foreign travel during 1989–90.

Note separately any important episodes linking events, or representing some longer cycle of change which you felt was taking place at the time. Having drawn and thought about his chart Neil, for example, noted the following episodes:

1981–84: 'Early apprenticeship' – building up confidence and skills in technical aspects of job and in relationships with partner and close work acquaintances.

1985–89: 'Facing up to reality' – the shine begins to wear off, jobs are not always what they seem at first, bosses are sometimes good, sometimes poor, but the bad patches have to be worked through. Start of a family brings new and potentially conflicting demands to be weighed against the pull and pressures of the job.

1989–92: 'Weathering the lows' – demands of job and family become more difficult to match with career, especially since starting an MBA programme. New job seemed disaster at first but beginning to feel good about coping with that and family tensions in ways that have strengthened marriage relationship.

(iii) Identify themes

When people work with their life-career charts in this way it is common for certain themes to persist or recur frequently. Look for themes in the account of your life to date. Spend time reflecting on the life-line you have plotted, digging beneath the surface of the incidents. Reflect on the material you have already unearthed in considering various perspectives on your managerial career and personal resources prompted by Chapters 2 and 3. Search for patterns of thoughts or feelings which might have accompanied or even triggered the various incidents you have plotted, especially associated with what you saw at the time as very significant events you might have labelled then as 'successes' or 'failures'. Having teased out these themes ask yourself if they are still 'hot' – do they continue to affect you in some way? If so, does it matter? Is it necessary to do something about it? Finally, what do you intend to do?

Since this is probably the most crucial and yet difficult step of plotting a life-line we give some examples of themes in Box 6.

Box 6
SOME OTHER PEOPLE'S THEMES

Gillian Ramsey, the personnel manager introduced on p. 53, had been a very promising pupil at school but decided not to go on to university, a decision she came to regret later. During her personnel career Gillian regularly did short courses of study of one sort or another and approached practical problems using a very effective blend of pragmatism and theory which tended to mark her out from more down-to-earth colleagues. On and off she began to consider moving into an academic career but could not decide whether this was motivated by a need to make up for the disappointment at having missed going to university or because of a genuine desire and potential flair for academic work. Eventually Gillian decided to tackle this theme by studying part-time for a first degree and then an MSc in Occupational Psychology. By the time she had finished the courses Gillian had decided that she did not, after all, want to become a full-time academic; instead, she left her personnel job to set up with two friends what was to become a very successful management

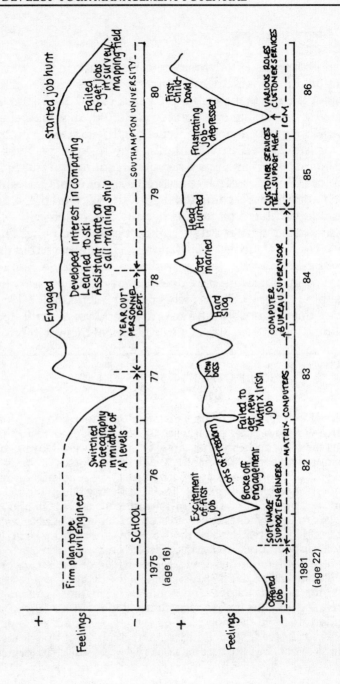

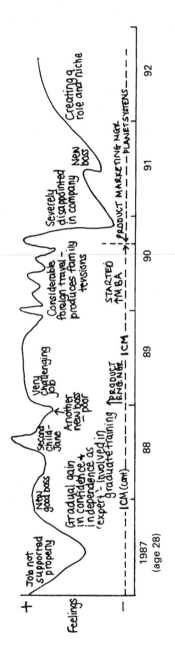

Figure 5 **Neil Compton – Life Career Chart**

consultancy. She also made room in a busy schedule to teach part-time on the MSc programme from which she had benefited earlier.

An important theme for Neil Compton has been about the nature of managerial work. From the time in his early twenties when he made a decision to try to become a manager the image he had in his mind was of controlling a group of people. This persisted well into his second job by which time he had been disappointed not to get a man-management job in Ireland, demoralised by the difficulties of supervisisng a systems group unwillingly providing a telephone back-up service, and frustrated at being rejected for a job as a field manager of a group of technicians installing communications equipment. Perhaps his focus on the top-down management relationship also accounted in part for the effect on him of various bosses, which he has noted in his lifeline. Gradually Neil has confronted this theme and built on his very high level technical skills to manage projects both from a systems development and a marketing standpoint. In the process he has come to realise that skills of influencing peers and bosses within a project framework are probably much more important than the skills of managing people in a high-technology sector where product and market development are so crucial.

Completing the portrait

Now, if you have followed all or some of the prompts so far in this and previous chapters, you should be in a position to complete a portrait of yourself as a manager, to place it into a frame of your full life, and to begin to see ways in which the portrait might be enhanced – probably by continuing to develop some existing life themes.

The materials for completing the portrait and beginning to plan changes should exist in your impressions of some or all of the following elements of your life so far:

(i)   A quite detailed sketch of yourself as a manager, including various key preferences, qualities, etc, and the personal resources of feeling, spirit and imagination which underpin those qualities.

(ii) How, through tackling various managerial jobs and meeting diverse challenges – including major achievements and failures – you have developed and grown in understanding to your current state.
(iii) Crucial relationships between aspects of your career as a manager and the life that you lead in other arenas.
(iv) Ideas about parts of the self-portrait as a manager which you would wish to change.
(v) How well you relate to others – for example, as colleague, friend, partner, parent and mentor – and what you contribute to other people's lives through those relationships.
(vi) What contribution you make to the wider community directly, or indirectly through family or work roles, and how you might wish to enhance that contribution in future.

Finally, in completing a current version of your self-portrait, consider who amongst those close to you – alive or dead – you would most want to appraise the outcome and any plans you make to change some of its features. Can you put yourself in their place and say how they might feel and what comments they might make?

Making plans

At this stage it should be possible to write down goals you still would like to reach, representing those parts of the current portrait you feel most strongly you wish to change. These could relate to any or all of the levels of your self, the arenas in which you are involved and the relationships you have in them – involving personal identity and resources, family and close friends, those at work, and in the wider community.

Because of this book's emphasis on your job and career as a manager these are likely to be the main focus of your planning. But the reason for placing the act of personal planning in a life-career frame is to try to ensure that, as a minimum, account is taken of the effect of career and job-related plans on other aspects of life. The optimum outcome, however, is if plans encompass quite deliberately and directly larger life themes concerning family and the wider community. Activities in any one arena and role are then more likely to enrich other facets of life and help in the development of a person who is able to contribute in many spheres.

Be realistic in deciding specific goals: it's much better to reach two or three comparatively minor goals than to collapse under the demands of achieving a number of major objectives. Like any exercise, physical or mental, build up your strength slowly. So prioritise the goals on two dimensions – their importance to you, and how achievable you think they are. Only you can decide which to fix on finally as part of a specific plan; other items can be included in later versions once priority issues have been tackled. This stage of choosing how to harness your energy to achieving personal change is, perhaps, the most important time to listen to the voice of the person you chose earlier to appraise your self-portrait and plans. What would he or she counsel?

If the situation you face at this stage seems intolerable then remember there are only three things you can do:

1. Change the situation.
2. Change yourself.
3. Leave the situation.

Some propose a fourth way out by changing the way you relate to the situation but this seems to us just the first step to changing yourself.

At this stage, as a check on your plans and to provide criteria against which to judge your success in realising them, imagine that you have been asked to write an obituary – for yourself! Do this in isolation from the plans you may have made but, again, take care to be realistic; remember that miracles do happen but not as a result of planning or wishful thinking. Share what you write with your friend, and then reconsider the plans in the light of what you've said in the obituary. If it's clear from reading it that you want people to have a certain image of you in memory, and that image is realisable, then do your plans correspond with its essential elements? If not, you might like to revise the plan yet again or re-write the obituary! And keep the obituary by you as a yardstick against which to measure the deeper significance for you of future accomplishments.

Chapter 5
Making Use of Opportunities
For Development

Introduction

In this chapter the focus and style changes considerably. We look forward, concentrating on how you can create and use opportunities for developing yourself in a way which is consistent with any plans you have begun to make. The chapter is in three sections:

(A) Personal development and the job cycle (p. 98)

We start by considering the importance of transitions into and out of jobs. After introducing the notion of a job cycle of experience we focus on three special development needs which occur during any transition:
- (i) Realistic previews of what to expect in the new situation.
- (ii) Informal feedback.
- (iii) Support from colleagues in overcoming difficulties encountered.

(B) Making use of development opportunities on offer (p. 109)

In the second section we examine various development opportunities presented by organisations to their managers at certain phases of their job or career, and the ways in which you might make better use of them if made available to you. The specific items are:
- (i) Formal performance appraisals.
- (ii) Education and training programmes.
- (iii) Succession plans.
- (iv) Special assignments.
- (v) Assessment centres.
- (vi) Personal development agreements.
- (vii) Ethics policies

(C) Self-management development (p. 130)
Here we underline the importance of self-managed
development and suggest some ways of following up this
key process by reference to books and articles on various
aspects including political skills, creative style and ethical
issues.

In the first section there are still a number of questions to
prompt you to consider various ways in which you might deal
with the stages of the job cycle. In the other two sections these
tend to give way to pieces of advice on how you might best
capitalise on development opportunities offered or which
could be created. As in the previous chapters questions are
introduced by the symbol ➤. Where we offer specific advice,
however, the symbol used is *.

(A) Personal development and the job cycle

Early on in Chapter 2 we reviewed briefly changes of
organisation and job, noting that the managers sampled in the
Managerial Survey changed jobs on average about every three
years. Some moved from one organisation to another
frequently too. Neil Compton, for example, moved to his
third organisation after only nine years' experience after
leaving university.

As we said earlier, there are no norms in moving jobs; nor
are there any in moving organisations: it's OK to move
organisations more or less frequently. Decisions of that sort
are a matter for individuals in the light of their own needs, the
opportunities which are presented, and the way in which
potential employers in the particular sector of the job market
might interpret their behaviour. There is no evidence that
people make successful careers just by staying with one
organisation, or by moving regularly. In the Managerial
Survey it was noted that some prosper by moving on; perhaps
temperamentally they are more restless and need to change.
Others prefer the stability of staying. On the other hand,

while some organisations prefer to develop their own managers and therefore recruit only young people, others introduce new blood at all levels, believing that newcomers provide a potential for organisational change.

Clearly there are limits: a very short period with any one organisation or in any one job gives little time for contributions to be made or for personal learning and development. And a record of frequent job moves can give an impression of restlessness and unreliability to a potential employer. This is likely to be especially marked in a sector which has enjoyed stability in employment patterns. By contrast, in a fast-moving sector such as computing, experiencing a shortage of skilled professionals and a pattern of high turnover, employers might not bat an eyelid. But, again, you must be the judge of the various issues, taking into account all of the circumstances at the time of any decision.

However frequently individual managers change job and organisation the transitions involved in those changes are usually crucial events in terms of the stress, the challenge and the development opportunities they present. And the stage at which managers are in their job cycle may have a considerable bearing on the opportunities for deliberate self-development. So we start this section by placing notions of development firmly within the stages of job cycles.

The model we use is that proposed by Nicholson and West, the authors of the Managerial Survey. They suggest a four-stage 'transition cycle' summarised in Figure 6. While the very 'neatness' of their model makes little allowance for the unplanned threats and opportunities which disturb the continuity of real life, we feel it provides a useful means of anticipating how transitions might be better managed.

In the *preparation/anticipation* stage people get ready for the change, imagining what the new job will be like and how well they will cope with the change.

The second stage is one of *encounter/shock* bringing a clash between what was anticipated and the reality of life in the new work environment. It can be a very traumatic and stressful stage but one which has its compensating stimulation, sense

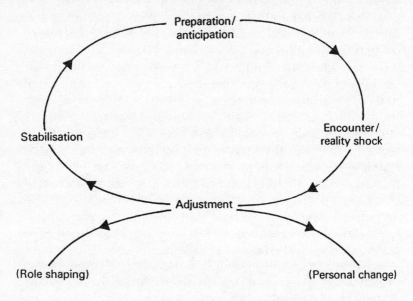

Figure 6 *The stages of the job cycle*

of hope and scope for exploration.

A process of *adjustment* takes place next as the manager tries to adapt to the new work demands and context. There can be two general sorts of outcomes: the individual's attitudes and behaviours change to fit the needs of the new situation (*personal change*), or the manager attempts to shape the environment, matching it more closely to personal interests, abilities, and goals (*role shaping*). While earlier we concentrated on role shaping, now we turn to questions of personal change.

The fourth and final stage, *stabilisation*, is a more settled period when the relationship between the individual and role can be fine tuned. Nicholson and West note that, if job tenure is generally as short as their research seems to indicate, most managers probably do not get far into this stage, if at all. This certainly seems true of Neil Compton.

Figure 7 shows the cycle elaborated with summaries of the

typical challenges and development questions which come with each stage. It is probable that the best opportunities to implement any personal plans come in the stabilisation stage when individuals typically focus on longer-term goals as they start looking for pastures new. But there is some scope throughout the cycle, as we shall see.

The concept of the job cycle is balanced between change and stability. It is important for individuals in the sorts of transitions studied in the Managerial Survey to be poised to respond to changing events internal and external to the organisation. As we have already seen there is a key link between experiencing the transitions of the cycle and learning. And as for the stress potentially involved, it is a question of finding the right level of comfort.

The descriptions in the figure are probably self-sufficient but we pick up on three crucial points in more detail: the need for a 'realistic preview' in the preparation stage and for feedback and support throughout the cycle but especially in the encounter and adjustment stages.

(i) Realistic preview

The key need is for as realistic a preview as possible of a new job in order to reduce the amount of shock when confronting the reality. Then you can be 'up and running' more quickly. This helps ensure that any stress is short-lived and containable and lays the basis for coping strategies which bring a sense of achievement in later stages and, with it, increased self-confidence and self-esteem.

Moving between organisations

Realistic preview is especially important when moving between organisations, but more difficult to achieve then. Neil Compton, for example, kicks himself for not insisting on meeting potential colleagues informally before taking his current job with Planet Systems. Given the chaos that he found on arrival he believes it is unlikely that some flavour of this would not have leaked out in discussion with existing members of the marketing group.

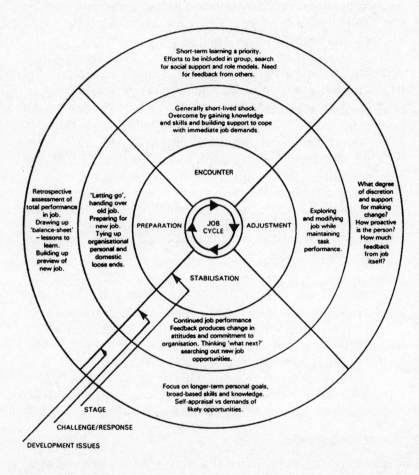

Figure 7 *Personal development and the job cycle*

Increasingly, the shortage of good quality professional recruits in some sectors is now beginning to hurt as fewer young people come onto the labour market and the demand for managers grows. One result is that more power is moving towards the recruit.

* So be prepared to take advantage of this. Many organisations already provide opportunities to meet potential colleagues. And if an organisation which is attempting to recruit you does not offer this as a matter of course then ask for meetings. Even a refusal on their part would be useful data and should cause you to reconsider the organisation's attractiveness as a place to work and develop.

* Don't rely on information provided by those doing the recruiting, however full it seems. Scan the business or technical press for comment. Any large reference library will give you access to information sources containing abstracts of the performance and fortunes of numerous companies. Try to get behind the quantitative data by finding out more about some of the key personalities and the stance they adopt on issues likely to affect you. For example, the *Financial Times, The Economist*, and many other quality newspapers and professional journals often contain articles about leading people in the field. They might have covered a senior manager in your target organisation recently. If so, does that person seem to represent the sort of values you could easily subscribe to?

* Better still, think of ways in which you might get an introduction to an existing manager or other professional who already works in the organisation.

Moving within an organisation

When moving within an organisation it is much easier to get a realistic preview.

* But, again, don't leave it to chance; make contacts for yourself through any network you have built up and follow up internal information sources. Staff of an internal library or information centre, or a planning department, may be

able to provide valuable data on distant departments or
locations for which you may be a potential recruit.

* If it is possible to find someone in the new department or
section who is seen as something of a 'villain' or 'clown'
they may have particularly interesting things to tell.
Individuals who don't fit into the mainstream of the
organisation, villains and clowns, pose some sort of
challenge to accepted goals and values. But they are likely
to be tolerated because of a special skill or just because
they have unusual and critical perspectives that may stop
others becoming complacent. Provided you take their
views with a 'pinch of salt', villains and clowns can provide
fascinating insights into people (they are hot on spotting
clay feet!) and situations. They may save you some nasty
surprises later.

(ii) Informal feedback

How can you get the amount of informal, 'on-the-job'
feedback which you feel you need?

In an ideal world your own manager should be providing
much of this spontaneously but in practice many managers
behave as if they haven't the time to talk to subordinates.
(Incidentally, how do *you* score on this point with the people
who work for you?) Certainly the managers in the survey
referred to earlier reported that they rarely received
structured or informal feedback. Neil Compton noted that
after two weeks with Planet Systems he had seen his boss for
only thirty minutes.

But why should the initiative always be downward? Why
not go and *seek* feedback?

* If you are in the encounter stage or early in the adjustment
stage of a job cycle and your boss hasn't yet agreed any
short-term goals with you, make some proposals yourself.
Once agreed you have then created a framework within
which to ask for regular feedback.

* But take care how you go about getting feedback, mainly by trying to understand and adapt to the style of your manager. If he or she is fairly straightforward and approachable then a question posed quite directly might yield useful feedback in the context, say, of a more general discussion of aspects of your job and its outputs. But if your boss shies away from personal questions, or prefers more indirect ways of dealing with them, then you have to contrive situations more carefully. Again, look for opportunities which occur within normal job-based exchanges, but try to create ways of eliciting feedback consistent with the preferred style.

And what is the image in the mirror like?

* If you have subordinates make sure to start a review process with them early in your own job cycle as their manager. This will benefit both them and you. For your part, finding out what they are currently doing will help you sort out the boundaries of your own job and alert you to critical tasks which you will need to monitor. And regular mutually-agreed sessions with them to monitor those key activities will provide feedback to you about your own style, coded perhaps but nonetheless real. In turn they may be flattered and encouraged by your early acknowledgement of the importance you place on a good working relationship with them.
* Similarly, regular meetings with peers, with whom your own role meshes, provide scope for building up relationships and, once this is done, for giving and receiving feedback.
* Other sources of feedback emerge from completion of the task – via clients, customers and other contacts or from performance indicators built into the task itself.

(iii) Support

In the encounter stage getting good support is as important as obtaining feedback, and of course the two are connected. We need support from people who can provide information and guidance, act as role models or lend a sympathetic ear. Some individuals are well supported by their bosses while others are neglected, especially if their manager is over-attentive to superiors. Neil Compton has experienced some interesting contrasts in this respect (see Box 7).

Box 7

NEIL COMPTON'S 'GOOD' AND 'BAD' BOSSES

In my first job with Matrix Computers I worked with *Ken* who was very competent technically. His easy way with customers gave me a useful role model at a time when I was sometimes overawed, having been dropped 'in the deep end' to look after a range of important customers including an airline, a police force, and a large bank. Ken was friendly, chatty and interested in what you were doing and talked regularly and at length with his colleagues. He was of imposing appearance – tall, long white hair, and wore an ammonite fossil as a pendant. When Ken and I worked together customers called us 'the wizard and his apprentice'.

Mark, my first boss in ICM, managed to give the impression of having your interests at heart, apparently sympathetic to staff concerns generally. He boosted morale by praise, etc, but rarely solved problems - personal, situational, or task. For example he was of little help to me in my efforts to manage a group of experienced technical people frustrated by being office-bound running a telephone support service.

Mark expected people to know what to do; he did not coach them to help make improvements. If he could not do certain tasks, or had no experience in one of the fields involved in our activity, he seemed intent on hiding this 'deficiency', especially from his superiors. Perhaps this made it difficult for him to work as an equal, in effect, with some of his people who were struggling in these same fields.

Overall Mark seemed very successful at positioning himself with respect to his bosses and opportunities which came along.

Helen was my second boss in ICM, concerned to understand what people wanted to do in their jobs and careers and to help them achieve it. She was very fair, fairer than the organisation in some ways, as when interpreting company policy on overseas travel to ease my lot during a difficult period of regular visits to the USA in 1987–8. This was an example of how she set the boundaries for you once she knew how you stood in relation to the organisation.

Helen also helped you sort out your own problems, using joint problem-solving to let me reach my own conclusions, coaching me as necessary through my thinking processes. Sometimes this led to outcomes which she probably anticipated. On other occasions an unexpected solution emerged and Helen would say 'that's interesting' and be prepared to spend time developing it. She worked hard at problem-solving, being able to think laterally and find answers to seemingly impossible questions. In those situations she coached me in the techniques which worked for her.

Helen's coaching and encouragement extended beyond the immediate problem. She helped me use the organisation's political system to get scarce resources and prompted me to improve presentations so that the aims and policies of the group were communicated more effectively, hence gaining the confidence of others on whom we relied.

Support from bosses

Ken and Helen served as role models for Neil in that they provided some standard of behaviour, even an ideal, which was worthy of imitation. Social psychologists argue that the imitation of a role model's behaviour is critical in helping to socialise people into new situations such as Neil found himself in at Matrix.

Certainly Helen acted as a coach, helping Neil to achieve better results on the job, not by direct instruction so much as through joint exploration of problems and the creation of opportunities for Neil to try out his new skills. Ambiguous situations were welcomed for the challenge they presented to puzzle things out. The result of Helen's coaching was that Neil felt more confident in his capacity to work independently.

Helen was probably a mentor, too, providing support for Neil in his efforts to develop himself and his career. He began to see Helen as a friend, someone he could bounce broader ideas off in attempts to resolve conflicts between his values and those of the organisation, between his job and other parts of his life, and between the present and the future. By the end of their time together Neil had become less concerned to find 'the solution'. Helen had helped him to become more tolerant of ambiguity, to accept it as natural, providing spice and variety in life.

As regards support from above how have you fared in your managerial career so far? The problem is that you don't choose your boss so it's difficult to plan for good ones! But like all relationships it's a two-way process so, as with feedback, you can take advantage of a good boss and make the best of a bad one by your own behaviour.

Some organisations appoint senior managers as coaches or mentors to young managers so that they don't have to rely on their immediate boss.

➤ Does your organisation have such an arrangement?
➤ If so, do you benefit from it? If not, what could you do to take advantage of what's on offer?

Perhaps your organisation doesn't have a coaching and mentoring scheme.

➤ If that's the case, could you influence your bosses to introduce one?

Alternatively, people often find coaches and mentors for themselves amongst senior colleagues they meet in day-to-day business or on training and other special programmes.

➤ If you have a need, how could you go about meeting it?

Should you be interested in taking the subject of coaching and mentoring further you might like to read an article on this topic by David Megginson.[1]

Although few who work outside worker co-operatives choose their bosses most managers have a hand in choosing their subordinates.

➤ How do you score in that direction? Do you provide better support to your people than did Mark, who head-hunted Neil into ICM?

➤ Can you learn from Ken or Helen? They seem to us to have a lot going for them as managers and colleagues.

Support from others

As for other sources of support, they are diverse. In a sense it depends on the direction of your task needs. If help is required from a technical department, or purchasing or accounts, and you approach them – humbly for advice or assertively with a strongly argued case that they should support your pet project – it is often surprising what people will do for you. Managers and other professionals in such departments often see their role as being to provide a service and can feel undervalued, so someone seeking their help, clearly with a genuine need, can be a form of emotional 'manna from heaven'.

Neil Compton got lots of support from colleagues in the personnel department at Matrix and ICM. This stemmed in part from his concern with problems of man management and, therefore, a felt need to understand personnel policies. But it may also have hinged on his own positive experience of working as an assistant in between school and university in a personnel department. No matter how you explain the links you make in this way, the important thing is to get the needed support.

(B) Making use of developmental opportunities on offer

In this section we look at formal opportunities which are often provided by organisations for their managers to enhance their development. Advice is provided on ways to make better use of formal performance appraisal systems; education and training programmes; succession plans; special assignments; assessment centres; personal development agreements; and ethics policies.

As we said at the beginning of the book, if the emphasis seems to be on large organisations then this is probably inevitable because, by and large, it tends to be the larger organisations that devote most attention to management development and the provision of formal programmes and opportunities for their managers. This has been confirmed in several recent surveys including the Managerial Survey. On the other hand, medium-sized and smaller organisations are being encouraged through various national initiatives to take a greater interest and make better provision. And one of the aims of our book is to encourage readers who work in those organisations to press for action to be taken. So, wherever possible we provide advice which covers such situations.

(i) Formal performance appraisal systems

Some organisations have formal systems for appraising and providing feedback on current performance and for assessing and planning to meet individuals' development needs (see Box 8). Formal appraisals are generally done on a yearly cycle although it is common for managers to be required to appraise employees after their first six months in a position.

Box 8

PERFORMANCE APPRAISAL SYSTEMS

Systems differ considerably from one organisation to another in the degree of sophistication, formality and control over their administration. Common features include:

Objective Setting
The appraisee's objectives are set or agreed mutually for the coming review period. Objectives might be quantitative (eg production or sales targets for a given period, generally a year) or qualitative (eg to make improvements such as a new procedure for monitoring bed-occupancy in a hospital, or introducing a new short course in a University management school).

Preparation for the Review
The appraiser and appraisee generally make separate preparations

---

for a review meeting to be held on a mutually agreed date at the end of the review period. Both assess progress against objectives, reasons for any special achievements or shortfalls, any development and training necessary to improve current performance and to prepare for future roles. This should incorporate key points raised in discussions about performance which have taken place regularly during the review period as part of the normal relationship on the job. At the same time the appraiser may be called on by the organisation to assess the appraisee's performance on some defined scale and may also be required as part of the process to indicate the appraisee's potential for more senior positions. This might take the form, for example, of an estimate of the most senior level at which the individual is considered likely to be able to perform effectively. In most systems appraisers are expected to get their manager's endorsement – as 'second reviewer' – of a written draft of the appraisal to be given to the appraisee.

Review Meeting
At the review meeting the appraiser gives an evaluation of performance with explanation. Similarly the appraisee provides a commentary and attempts are made to resolve any gross discrepancies between the two accounts. The aim is to arrive at some mutually agreed assessment although the appraisee is free to lodge objections to the scaled performance and the appraiser's comments. Usually, potential for further promotion is commented on, if at all, in very general terms on the grounds that to do otherwise might cause the appraisee to have unrealistic expectations. Tentative development and training plans are agreed for the next review period, taking account as far as possible of the appraisee's views on his own needs. Finally, revised objectives are agreed for the next review period.

Follow-up
The manager may be required to follow up in several ways:
(i) By progressing independently any agreed actions which can be taken on the job or within the training budget.
(ii) By making proposals for the appraisee to be included in any organisation-wide training programmes or other development initiatives (such as assessment centres, discussed below) and advising the appraisee of any decisions made.
(iii) By feeding data on performance and potential assessments into any financial reward and succession planning systems (see below).

What can you do to improve your own development opportunities in cases where a formal appraisal system operates? We suggest you consider the following:

Preparation
* Think very seriously about your objectives for the following period. If your boss does not give you sufficient notice of the review meeting to enable you to do this satisfactorily, and to summarise your own impressions of performance during the previous period, seek to defer the meeting so this can be done. In this way you are less likely to agree to unrealistic quantitative targets or to make qualitative changes to the job that do not square with your own views of what is necessary or realistic. You are much more likely to shine when working towards objectives to which you are committed.

* Consider using an abbreviated form of the personal planning process we have followed in the previous three chapters to prepare for the review, especially if it comes during the more stable stage of a job cycle when you are beginning to consider new job opportunities. After the first time you do it a personal plan only needs updating on a regular basis with occasional more fundamental revisions at crucial job or career milestones. By this means you will be in the best position to influence decisions made to meet your development and training needs, including the types of future job experience you would prefer.

* If you work in an organisation which plans in any detail the job moves of managers there will be times, as you clarify your own career objectives, when it will be important to know as clearly as you can what the organisation has planned for you. Even if specific plans are not drawn up you may wish to know how highly regarded you are as a potential manger in more senior positions. So prepare to press your manager about the assessment of your potential and what plans have been made to move you to other positions in line with any earlier discussions. We will return to this topic under 'succession planning'.

Ongoing Informal Reviews
* Make sure as far as you can that progress against objectives is regularly reviewed informally during the review period. You can then seek to have the targets changed as necessary in the light of experience (eg reduced, because resources necessary for their achievement are not available). Just as important, it is less likely that there will be big gaps to be bridged at the formal review meeting between your account of performance during the previous period and that of your manager.

Follow-up
* Follow up promised actions. Fix what you can yourself. Then press your boss to fix dates for agreed activities, such as informal review meetings or short-term assignments in other roles within the group. Ask to be told as soon as decisions are made to include you in organisation-wide programmes. Keep on asking for information.
* If necessary, get your boss to explain the connection between the scaled performance appraisal and any financial rewards (see Box 9). When those rewards result from, say, a formal basic salary or bonus system check that the salary increment or bonus is in line with what your manager told you. If there appears to be a discrepancy seek a clarification so that you can sort it out together.

Again, look in the mirror:

➤ Do the people for whom you are the appraiser need to use such tactics to get you to deliver your side of the bargain? Or do you follow the spirit of the system? How can you improve your performance?

Introducing an Appraisal System
* If there is no formal appraisal system what can you do? Start by appraising those who report to you. You can also attempt to persuade your boss to run an informal local system (loosely along the lines of those in Box 8) just for you or the whole group supervised. Start with objective setting and regular impromptu reviews of progress against those. This can lead naturally into discussions of your development needs. Fancy forms and back-up systems are not needed for a simple local system of this sort.

Box 9
PERFORMANCE-RELATED REWARD SYSTEMS

Private enterprise companies have traditionally had formal systems linking financial rewards to assessed performance. Many more organisations, including those in the public sector, are being encouraged to introduce such systems as part of a general 'sharpening up of accountability' and in an attempt to enhance 'employee commitment'. It is a central premise of human resource management that the financial reward system should support the overall organisation's values and objectives. For example, in an organisation where great value is placed on serving the customer many of the overall and individual managers' objectives are likely to relate to this need. So, a person's achievements which serve the customer best will probably be given a heavy weight in the assessment of performance and in the financial reward decisions triggered by the assessment.

In performance-related salary systems all or part of an individual's earnings are related in some way to assessed performance. In those organisations which have a regular, formal review of salary levels it is common for the salary increment which any individual gets to be related to performance on the basis of some simple formula.

For example, in a review of salaries based on a planned average increment of 4% and a five-point scale of performance, the top management may lay down the following relationship (where a '1' performance is, high, '5' is low):

Performance level:	1	2	3	4	5
Salary increase (%) planned by level:	16	8	4	2	0

Although the average increase is 4% of salary, a 'top performer' might get as much as 16% while the 'bottom performer' could get no increment at all.

(ii) Education and training programmes

This section might have been headed: 'Beware of manager bearing gifts', because some managers offer training programmes as a gift to make up for something else. Neil

Compton, for example, was 'sent' on a month's training programme at a prestigious management college just after his disappointment at not being selected for a job as manager of a field installation group. He enjoyed the 'month off', meeting the other people on the course, the cuisine, and the general ambience of the college in its acres of parkland. But he was left wondering what it was all about, not sure what – if anything – he had learned and, if he had learned anything, how it related to his job.

How can you avoid the same pitfall? For a start:

➤ Do you have some sort of picture of your own current needs to improve skills or acquire knowledge?

➤ And can you place these needs within a broader framework of more general life and career aims?

If so, you should be able to look at the prospectus for a training programme or more extended course of education and decide whether it is likely to help you meet your needs. And if you can do that it will be easier to refuse managers' 'gifts' of courses to go on. At least you will have some rationale which they should be able to relate to!

Even if you do decide, independently or in consultation with your manager, that you wish to take an extended programme of manager education and development such as a DMS or MBA there is considerable choice in terms of part-time or full-time; day attendance or residential; theoretical or practical; conventional design or modular design; and so on. In Part III we set out some of the key options to consider when choosing programmes which lead to the award of a formal qualification, and provide guidance on making choices.

(iii) Succession plans

Appraisal systems can also lead naturally into succession plans. Some organisations, especially larger and more bureaucratic ones, use the data drawn from performance appraisals to try to ensure that there is an adequate supply of potential managers to fill the expected number of managerial positions at various levels in the future. See Box 10 for more detail.

Box 10

SUCCESSION PLANS

Many organisations do not attempt to plan management succession, even in the most general sort of way. Even where plans are made they vary considerably in principle and detail from one organisation to another.

Where an organisation is in a rapidly changing environment and flexibility is crucial, or where informality is a key value, any succession plans are likely to be in very general terms. Without attempting to predict which current management positions will exist in the future, a plan might be based on a forecast of the number of positions at various levels. An analysis is made, based on the assessed managerial potential of current employees, to show the likely surplus or shortfall of managers at the various levels at future dates. Finally, the plan sets out actions to be taken to deal with the predicted situation. For example, to meet a shortfall, recruitment targets might be increased and development programmes for existing managers be accelerated.

Such an overall plan might be backed up with broad development plans for selected managers. These could show how many levels the individual is expected to rise through the hierarchy in a certain time-scale and indicate some typical sort of mix of development experience required in the interim (eg by function and type of experience – planning, manufacturing, overseas assignment, etc). Actual decisions are then made to meet specific needs created by short-term events such as organisational change, a resignation, etc.

In more stable organisations or those with a preference for more formality, plans might be made for filling specified positions. Managers judged currently to have the potential to get to a certain position are listed against that position without differentiating between them. Alternatively, they might be ranked in order of probability of getting there; and some may be shown as ready for the position soon (eg in the next two years) with others listed as likely to be ready later. Similarly, development plans for individuals in a more formal system might show a list of positions to which they are expected to progress on current assessments of performance and potential.

➤ In this context, how can you influence things?

To start with, do you know whether your organisation has a succession planning system? You may, for example, already be involved in preparing plans for others.

* Try to make sure that you have a thorough understanding of how the system works both for your sake and those who work for you. (In our experience the fact that managers are involved in preparing specific position and development plans does not mean that they automatically have a good picture. Such an aura of secrecy can surround the planning process that all but the most senior actors know only their lines, not the whole 'play'.)

* If you believe that the organisation is likely to have developed a plan for you, still try to maintain control of events. Do all you can to find out about the plan and compare what it envisages with any outline plans you have made for your own career. Winkle out information if necessary by saying, 'What I fancy doing is this; how does that square with the plan?'. Even a manager who 'keeps mum' may still take what you say into account.

But don't overdo pressure of this sort; use it sparingly for occasions when you need to know more in order to make crucial decisions.

(iv) Special assignments

In most organisations from time to time there are opportunities to do a 'special assignment': a short period of stand-in for someone off sick or on a course; a project to achieve a specific objective on your own or working as a member of a project group; or, more exotic still, an overseas assignment to fill a regular position or to join a special project in an associated company. Such situations can be a hard test of life and career plans. If your plans are very firm and the assignment as described doesn't match up to them then you may feel obliged to turn it down. But to do so might risk your missing a chance to develop in unexpected directions, to perform well in a very new context with high visibility, to give your family a once-in-a-lifetime experience. By contrast, if you have no plan or a very poor one, or if you flex your plan too willingly under your manager's pressure to 'take your chances', then a few months later might find you in the back-of-beyond reflecting over the sixth beer 'Why the hell am I here?'.

There is probably little more we can do than point out the possible dilemmas. These can stem from your personal work and immediate career needs; the needs of your partner and any children; and how flexible you and your partner can be in the circumstances. But if you do decide to accept an assignment then the same sorts of issues will arise which we covered earlier under realistic previews, informal feedback, and support.

* If the assignment involves a move to another location, insist on visiting it and meeting people there first. Take your family, especially if they are to relocate with you.
* For foreign assignments some organisations arrange extensive induction programmes to introduce their assignees to the traditions, culture, laws, etc, and the more mundane everyday conditions likely to be experienced in the host country. Find out if your organisation does this. If not, try to get a special package for you and your family: they are provided for most countries by external training organisations.
* Where your partner wishes to relocate but would prefer to continue to work try to ensure that your employer helps him or her secure a suitable job. Increasingly this is an issue for people locating and there is evidence that employers are much more willing to go out of their way to help, sometimes by finding jobs for partners in the overseas affiliate organisation.
* Even if you do not expect to gain financially from the assignment try to make sure at least that you are not out of pocket through the move and that your salary and benefit position (especially pension) is safeguarded back home.
* You will be helped in this if, for the period of assignment away from your normal base, you try to keep in touch. Make

regular contacts with one or more close colleagues to tune in from a distance to any important grapevine and, especially, to find out about changes which may affect you directly. Arrange to receive copies of internal communications to all managers, of regular house journals and of other general employee communications likely to be of interest.

(v) Assessment centres

Appointments to managerial positions made on the basis of ongoing assessments of performance are typical of many organisations. Potential is estimated by observing how individuals perform in real-life jobs. Other organisations supplement this, in effect, by using a short burst of synthetic experience called an 'assessment centre' (see Box 11). It is used to:

● Select recruits to the organisation
● Select for promotion to a specific position.
● Select for inclusion in an accelerated development programme for 'high fliers'.
● Audit the capabilities of the management population.
● Provide developmental experience to those taking part, sometimes as an introduction to a personal planning process.

Box 11

ASSESSMENT CENTRES

In an assessment centre, candidates are placed in a series of simulated managerial situations so that their behaviour can be observed and an assessment made of their potential as managers. The practice, originally called an extended interview, was first used in the German army in the 1930s and was developed by the Allied armed services during the Second World War. Currently it is extensively used in the USA and is becoming increasingly popular in Britain, mainly among larger companies.

Three basic assumptions underpin the practice:

(a)   That it is possible to identify and measure 'dimensions' of performance (eg problem analysis, judgement, decisiveness, persuasiveness) on which individuals should score highly if they are to perform well as managers in the target organisation.
(b)   That psychological tests and exercises can be devised which can be used to assess the extent to which a candidate demonstrates these dimensions of performance.
(c)   That observers can be trained to make the assessment by observing how candidates perform on the exercises.

A group of individuals spend up to several days together, submitting themselves to psychological tests, being interviewed by managers trained to act as assessors, and taking part in various individual and group exercises under the eye of those same assessors. The exercises typically include such things as:

- 'In-basket', where each candidate is given time to play a general manager's role in dealing with memos, letters, reports and other documents gathered from real-life examples.
- Leaderless group discussion.
- Preparation of a plan to achieve some defined goal.
- Leading of a group to implement that plan.

Not all of the exercises tap every dimension under review but, together with interview findings, they are intended to provide a composite coverage of the set of dimensions.

The data from interviews, tests and exercises is reviewed and discussed by the group of assessors. In the most formal contexts this involves each assessor rating each candidate on each of the dimensions and, on the basis of these ratings, allocating an overall assessment rating. The group then discusses the separate and overall ratings for each candidate in order to arrive at a consensus overall rating. Results of psychological tests are not usually made available to the assessors until after consensus ratings have been agreed or, in some cases, to help assessors who are finding difficulty in arriving at a consensus.

Soon afterwards candidates are debriefed by one of the assessors about their performance and whether they have been selected or not. In programmes intended to aid development rather than selection the individual taking part is counselled at this stage on what might be done to build on strengths and overcome any weaknesses in performance. Counselling may also form part of the debriefing after assessment programmes used mainly for selection.

Some organisations have the practice, which we like, of running a short workshop for the assessors after the assessment centre is over to help them concentrate on what they have learned about assessment of performance and the process of giving feedback.

To date assessment centre programmes have been used largely for selection. But there is a view, which we share, that programmes are increasingly being used to provide developmental experience. To compensate for the shortfall of good quality recruits available in the 1990s, we expect the more progressive organisations to place considerable emphasis on making better use of the people they have, especially those with managerial experience and potential. In this context assessment centres are becoming 'development centres' used not just to assess potential but to help those attending to recognise and develop their own potential. Such a trend underlines further the establishment of self-managed learning as individuals take responsibility for their own learning and development with the support of the organisation.

If your organisation does not use assessment centres then, perhaps, this section has little relevance for you. On the other hand:

* You might be interested and be in a position to suggest that they be considered for use in your organisation.

You might also apply for jobs elsewhere in the future. If an assessment centre is used as part of the selection process then:

* In building up a realistic preview of the situation, try to get a feel for how the programme is run and what exercises are included. Even if you have experienced assessment centre programmes before, prepare yourself by getting as much information as you can on the one you are about to experience, preferably from someone who has experienced it.

If assessment centres are used in your organisation and you are about to take part in one them:

* You should more easily be able to get a preview from colleagues or by chasing up people from elsewhere in the organisation. It's worth talking to more than one to get alternative viewpoints.

If you haven't yet been invited to take part in an assessment centre and feel you would like to then:

* Lobby your boss. Managers might have to press for their subordinates to be included and yours may not be fully aware of access to assessment centres. In that case you and your colleagues could be losing out and your approach will be to everyone's advantage.

Where the centre is used for selection for advanced development programmes or as a development experience in itself you will be in a stronger position to persuade your manager to nominate you if you have some sort of personal plan as proposed in Chapter 4.

Should you take part in an assessment programme, probably the most important advice we can give is:

* Avoid unnecessary competition with other candidates where the centre is part of a selection process. The experience is likely to be stressful enough as it is: don't add to the burden. Be assertive and 'keep your end up', but avoid scoring points off others. In fact, we'd suggest quite a different tactic. What you will probably benefit from most is the support of the others during the few genuinely informal situations when you can relax. Sharing views on events you have experienced will help you all understand better what is happening as a basis for improved personal performance.
* Where the programme is used solely for development purposes then this sharing of experiences will be an essential part of the process. Make the best of it; in even a medium-sized organisation you may not meet many of these people again. They have something to give you, and vice versa, in a very short, precious period of time.
* Make sure you get a good debriefing. Even if it is a selection

programme, where the assessor's main aim is to decide 'yes' or 'no', find out as much as you can about the rating given. Probe to get the assessor's views on what you might learn from this, how you might plan to build on strong points and improve on others. Ask for comments on any embryo personal plans.

* If it is a development programme then the debriefing should be intended to provide direction and impetus for you in improving your own performance. Depending on who does the debriefing, consider discussing with that person your own preliminary plans for personal development as a basis for eventually building into them whatever you may learn from the assessment.

(vi) Personal development agreements

It is quite probable that organisations who use assessment centre programmes for development purposes will also be interested in 'personal development agreements', also called 'personal learning contracts' or 'management learning contracts.' The personal development agreement (PDA) defines an explicit understanding about an individual's learning goals and how these might be met, arrived at between that person and a manager or trainer acting on behalf of the organisation. In Box 12 we list the main features of the more sophisticated forms of PDA. You may find in practice, that if an organisation uses PDAs they are considerably simpler than this.

Box 12
PERSONAL DEVELOPMENT AGREEMENTS

Aims and Broad Principles
There are two main categories of agreement:

- 'Level one' PDAs are intended to help the individual improve job performance and skills. Current development needs are identified and agreement reached on how these can be met. Organisations probably see the relevance of PDAs at this level to all types of employee from truck driver to managing director.

PDAs are concerned with how to further the
nt of life and career goals. A crucial part of the
nt is the role of the organisation and its agents in
ng individuals to make progress toward their goals.
anisations might consider level two PDAs of relevance
only to key individuals and people at crossroads in their
careers.

PDAs symbolise the value placed on an organisation's members,
showing that those with the power to do so are prepared to invest
time and resources in facilitating learning and development. Also
implicit is the notion of self-managed learning which is assumed
throughout this book. Hence PDAs emphasise individual
responsibility for learning with support from the organisation.
Self-managed learning, the argument goes, engages the
individual's will and therefore is an effective route to real change.

Process
The process of arranging a PDA has seven steps:

(a) Selection — who should work through the process.
(b) Preparation— diagnosing needs and setting goals using various approaches including inventories of learning style or skill, career planning guides and structured discussion.
(c) Exploration — mapping out key issues.
(d) Planning — deciding how, when, and by whom agreed needs will be met. A key part of the plan is a list of resources to be made available.
(e) Contracting— reaching a clear agreement on what the various parties will do by when. This will include success criteria and measures for judging progress against the plan.
(f) Assessing — assessing performance against the plan and modifying as necessary.
(g) Recording — setting up and maintaining a personal and organisational record of progress.

If you are fortunate enough to work in an organisation
where PDAs are already used then you might consider the
following suggestions:

* If you believe that a level two PDA is something you might benefit from in the light of your own career plans press your manager to include you, even if he has initially decided that you don't fit the category of 'key individuals and people at crossroads in their careers' (see Box 12).
* You will improve your case and be better prepared to take advantage of a PDA if you do your homework well in clarifying life and career aspirations and identifying personal development needs. So this might be a crucial time to work through Chapters 2 to 4 again or to follow up the leads we offer below to more detailed sources for self-managed learning. However enlightened the management is, your interests will probably be served best by doing a deep preliminary review for yourself, using independent counsellors as necessary. Then you will be well placed to take good advantage of the preparation and counselling stages of the PDA process within the organisation.

Even if your organisation does not use PDAs as a matter of policy we suggest you:

* Ask your boss to enter into one specially for you. If you already know a trainer in the organisation, or someone else who could help you and your manager work through the process, then that would probably help to sell and develop the idea.

Finally, you might be in a position to influence organisational policy by:

* Suggesting that PDAs be introduced on a widespread basis. If so, and you are seeking help, consider reading George Boak's book on the management learning contract[2]. While this tends to concentrate on what we have called level one PDAs and emphasises too much the role of trainers in the process, it provides very detailed advice, backed up with case studies, on the steps listed in Box 12. Alternatively you can contact one of the organisations listed at the end of the book.

(vii) Ethics Policies

You might be asking what 'ethics policies' have got to do with management development within an organisation. For us the reason lies in our introductory comments about the purpose of managerial effectiveness, about the need for some moral vision which sustains all members of organisations and not just those formally appointed as managers. Without such a vision and some sort of ethical framework within which it can be sustained it is difficult to imagine that people will have the freedom of speech and action which is central to personal development and to protecting the organisation's good name.

Increasingly, this seems to be the position being taken up, too, by the leaders of many British businesses. They are recognising the need to ensure that their organisations are ethically self-regulating if society is to continue to grant them the freedoms which, they claim, are necessary for commercial success — to choose what to produce and supply; to decide who to associate with; to have limited liabilities; to charge consumers the costs of research and development; and to hire and fire. And if self-regulation is to cover ethical questions it must mean not just obeying the law but ensuring that 'businesses aim also to be good places to buy from, to sell to, to work in, to invest in, and increasingly to be good neighbours, ie to take account of the effect on others of their actions or inactions'[3].

Some of the specific points which might make up a policy for ethical self-regulation are covered in Box 13.

Box 13

COMPONENTS OF AN ETHICS POLICY

The survey carried out by Marlene Winfield among British businesses, reported in her 1990 book *Minding Your Own Business*, enabled her to identify from good company practice the following components out of which an ethical policy might be constructed:

- A corporate philosophy and strategy with specific ethical elements.
- A business mission which clearly links ethical behaviour, strategy, values and purpose.
- A code of ethics setting out general priorities for business goals backed up by a code of practice providing specific guidance, clarified as and when required.
- Facilities for all employees to participate in a culture in which they are encouraged to raise ethical issues and are protected from any reprisals when they do so.
- The adaptation of decision making procedures to allow for the ethical dimension of all decisions and the particular concerns of employees.
- Processes for monitoring the working of the ethical policy.

Perhaps the most important issue both in general terms and especially in the context of self-development is the recognition that, in the end, the individual employee is the most important but neglected resource in ensuring that self-regulation is taken seriously inside and outside the organisation. People who depend on a business to behave well towards them depend essentially on its members — their words and actions provide reassurance that the freedoms granted to their organisation will not be abused. In the introduction to Winfield's book, John Banham, then Director General of the Confederation of British Industry, stressed the importance of 'self-regulation based on an understanding of employees' value to the business, their needs and problems'. Clear guidelines are required 'on the rights and expectations of employees and of management with clear rules to assist in day to day conduct at work'. Unfortunately, guidelines alone are not enough and rules can create bureaucratic nonsenses such as the need to obtain three tenders for trivial amounts of expenditure on behalf of the organisation. Crucial is the active commitment of management to resolving ethical issues: in Banham's words management must 'give support to employees who report wrong-doing which is damaging the company. These "whistleblowers" should be regarded as a safety net where other forms of regulation fail, and meritorious "whistleblowers" protected'.

* Against this background we suggest that you recall any notes you made earlier about personal values as compared to your perception of corporate values. You might now wish to consider how they contrast in the context of ethical issues — an invitation to reflect on how you might help the organisation to become an even better 'corporate citizen'.

➤ If the organisation has an ethics policy how does it square with the components recommended by Winfield in Box 13?

➤ If there is no ethics policy does this matter? Perhaps the organisation's culture is such that you and your colleagues feel confident that the essence of such a policy is implicit. In that case, how can you make sure that competitive and other pressures don't cause the moral vision to be compromised?

➤ If, on reflection, ethical issues tend to be neglected in spirit and practice is it important for you to do so something about it?

* Whether you take up a specific ethical issue which is bothering you, now or in the future, is up to you. But if ever you do decide that such a step is necessary consider the following advice provided by Marlene Winfield:

  • **Prepare yourself mentally** by checking your motives and whether the public interest is really at stake; by being realistic in assessing the effects on the organisation and yourself; and, while remaining optimistic, being prepared for defeat.

  • **Prepare your case well** by identifying and prioritising the issues carefully; being able to quote relevant laws, professional codes of practice and organisational guidelines; and by documenting the evidence to check that you are right.

  • **Exhaust internal channels first** based on an action plan, making sure that you document the actions taken; remain flexible and patient, giving the organisation time to respond to your representations.

- **Protect yourself** by trying to enlist internal support and finding someone more senior you can trust as a sounding board; behaving and performing well throughout; and knowing your legal rights. Be mindful also of the extent to which you may be risking your job security or long term career prospects.
- **Go outside only if there is no alternative;** but if you do, go through a person or group who might be able to provide some degree of protection; focus on issues and not personalities; and record everything that happens particularly at work.

Reading this advice it must be clear that whistleblowing is a risky step to take with no assurance that any of the parties — individual, organisation or community — will be judged a winner. This is why we support the introduction of ethics policies in reducing the need for whistleblowing seen as threatening to the organisation and in providing protection for those whose consciences still bring them to take action.

Against this sobering assessment no one is going to stand in judgment on an individual's development, especially on the profound and confusing issues of personal choice implied, where questions far outnumber any known answers. Each of us has to wrestle with our conscience and find ways of balancing responsibilities between our family and close friends, colleagues and others within and outside the organisation. Perhaps it is some comfort to consider ourselves as just the latest of a broad stream of individuals in history who have struggled with the most perplexing and painful of dilemmas: how to lead a good life in a social world where shades of grey are much more common than black and white.

For this reason we would welcome your views on this aspect of personal and community development perhaps more than on any of the other issues raised in this section of the book. On the other hand, if you are seeking to follow up for your own purposes any of the points raised here and elsewhere you might care to read some of the references which follow or to contact organisations listed at the end of the book, especially AMED and the Institute of Personnel Management.

(C) Self-managed development

A good way of closing this part of the book is to re-focus on the whole notion of self-managed development and learning. One of our key assumptions has been that you will be keen to manage your own development. On the other hand, it must be clear that we have only just scratched the surface. So, in case you want to dig deeper – because of a need to be more independent of your organisation despite the formal scope it offers for development, or because you don't have that level of organisational support – then you might like to use the following sources on which we drew in Chapters 2 to 4.

(i) General sources

There are three general books we recommend:

1. *Managing Yourself* by Mike Pedler and Tom Boydell (Fontana Paperbacks, London, 1985).
    This book is aimed at individuals who are aware that things are changing, that the energy and creativity of the whole person needs to be freed if, collectively, we are to face up to the technical, social and political challenges of the end of the twentieth century.
    Readers are encouraged to engage in a lively process of exploration, analysis, deciding and taking action as they progress through the following sections of the book:
    - In the first chapter various models of self-management are introduced which are developed in more detail in the next five chapters: getting things done; knowing yourself; valuing and being yourself; being skilful; managing your health.
    - Chapter 7 moves outward, covering working with other people.
    - Chapter 8 focuses on managing yourself within the organisation.

2. *A Manager's Guide to Self-Development* (2nd Edition) by Mike Pedler, John Burgoyne and Tom Boydell (McGraw-Hill, Maidenhead, 1986).

The authors' fundamental premise is:

'that any effective system for management development must increase the manager's capacity and willingness to take control over and responsibility for events, and particularly for themselves and their own learning.' (p 3)

They believe that much of the effort put into formal management development programmes and writing has had the effect of de-skilling managers by encouraging them to believe that, whatever the problem, an expert is available, and that experts in management development can manage our learning as managers for us. So Pedler, Burgoyne and Boydell see their book as providing an antidote, a vehicle for managers to help themselves increase their 'capacity and willingness to take control over, and responsibility for, events' (p 4).

This they do through:

- a life-career planning activity, similar to the one used in Chapter 4 above.
- self-assessment and goal setting against a portfolio of a successful manager's qualities which overlaps with that used in Chapter 3 above.
- forty-two detailed activities which can assist in self-development and a guide to how to select from those activities depending on the needs identified in the process of self-assessment. Activities include making contacts, managing your time, decision-making, planning change, action planning, approaches to creativity, understanding your learning processes, and study skills.

3. *Working Choices – A Life-planning Guide for Women* by Jane Skinner and Rennie Fritchie (Dent, London, 1988).

Jane Skinner and Rennie Fritchie take the same basic position as the authors of this and the two other books, that people need to plan and take charge of their own lives. For women, however, they argue that this need is all the more important because of the disadvantages they tend to face in our society. But the book 'is not about developing a new breed of super successful business women who dedicate their whole lives to work. It is about learning more about who you are, what choices you can make and how to increase your chances of getting what you want' (p 4).

The focus is on how to benefit from changes taking place in the 1990s which seem to offer more scope for women to make use of their advantages 'that will help them be creative and will act to make changes work for them' (p 12). To help women benefit in this way Skinner and Fritchie offer the following path through their book, based on regular exercises for the reader to do:

(a) Taking stock of who you are now, leading to what new horizons may be opening up.
(b) Getting started on issues of 'you' and 'work' ending up with an exploration of personal attitudes and talents.
(c) Developing skills important for a broad and balanced life and for getting into work and getting on at work. Topics covered include managing interviews, building good relationships, developing meeting skills, being assertive and handling stress.
(d) Understanding patterns and pathways by examining women's biographies as an aid to life and career planning.

(ii) Some specific skills

Apart from the general questions of self-managed development covered in these books you might be interested in specific areas which we dealt with briefly in Chapters 2 and 3. So, finally, we offer some pointers to where you can get help concerning political skills, creative style and ethical issues.

(a) Political skills

None of the three books referred to above devotes much attention directly to the development of political skills. If this is an area in which you are particularly interested then consider reading the book by Larry Greiner and Virginia Schein on *Power and Organization Development*, published in 1989 by Addison Wesley. Their focus on power and politics is broader than ours, tending to concentrate on the role of consultants and other 'change agents' mobilising power to create organisational change, but the first part of their book gives a very readable account aimed at the practising manager.

Alternatively you might like to use the full questionnaire dealing with 'Four factors shaping power and influence' which we also introduced in Chapter 2. Apart from the three aspects of a manager's job on which we focused there – visibility, autonomy, and relevance – the questionnaire, designed by Goodmeasure, of Cambridge, Massachusetts, also covers the relationships that are important in shaping power and influence.

A copy of the questionnaire and brief notes on how to use it are contained in the book:

Creative Organization Theory, by Gareth Morgan (Sage, California, 1989).

(b) Creative style

Many organisations and individuals have written books, or offer training, on the enhancement of various skills involved in creative activities. Recommended books are:

Adams, J L (1988) *The Care and Feeding of Ideas*, Harmondsworth: Penguin.
de Bono, E (1986) *Lateral Thinking for Managers*, Harmondsworth: Penguin.
Rickards, T (1988) *Creativity at Work*, Aldershot: Gower.

(c) Ethical issues and policies

Marlene Winfield, in *Minding Your Own Business*, provides a short but comprehensive account of her study into business ethics illustrated with some fascinating, if sometimes chilling, personal case histories. If you wish to read further still she provides an extensive reading list. Details of her book are given below.

This brief review of some key sources in the area of self-managed development concludes the second part of the book. If there are particular avenues you wish to explore then these sources and the notes at the end of each of the chapters should provide a rich variety of leads. Otherwise you might like to contact AMED who could put you in touch with one or more members who specialise in the various fields.

Notes

1. Megginson, D (1988) 'Instructor, coach, mentor: three ways of helping managers', in the journal *Management Education and Development*, vol 19(1).
2. Boak, G (1991) *Developing Managerial Competences: The Management Learning Contract*, London: Pitman.
3. Winfield, M (1990) *Minding Your Own Business*, London: Social Audit, p 4.

Part III Cutting Through the Qualification Maze

Cutting Through the Qualification Maze

Introduction

This section concentrates mainly on qualification courses. This is because, in this sphere, the person who makes the decision to attend is *you*. The personal commitment you have to make is considerable in terms of time and effort. It may also cost you a considerable amount of money. There are other courses of anything between 3 and 12 weeks, which, although they give no qualification, require a large effort from you. It is highly unlikely, however, that you would go on one of these programmes if your employer were not paying. So we have concentrated on providing guidance on qualifications. Even so, there is some guidance later in this chapter about management courses more generally. The general comments on style and content are equally applicable to almost any course and you may therefore find it useful to consider them if your employer offers you any 'open' course, ie one which draws participants from several organisations.

In general, the section aims to help you to decide the following:

- Is it worth my while taking a business or management qualification?
- If so, what sort of qualification should it be?
- What should I expect and how can I get the best from it?

It is probably best to start this process by giving you a picture of what is on offer. We will then look at how the picture is changing. We will show how courses with the same name can vary from place to place, give you some more details on the main qualifications, and finally take you through some of the key criteria for making a decision.

What is on offer?

The picture is confusing because there are several different qualifications on offer and a range of medium-length non-qualification courses aimed at different levels of managerial responsibility and for people with varying amounts of work experience and previous academic qualifications. They may use 'business' or 'management' in their titles.

Perhaps the best known qualification is the MBA, the Master of Business Administration. The degree originated in the United States, was imported into the UK in the 1960s and its use has been steadily growing in Europe and other parts of the world ever since. This growth has not, however, been at the same rate in different countries. If you see your future as being in a country other than the United Kingdom, or for an organisation based outside the UK, you would be well advised to investigate the prevalent attitude to the MBA. You should also bear in mind that in certain countries, for example Japan, there is a greater importance attached to management training being related specifically to an organisation's needs and hence sponsorship. While you may feel that the skills associated with having an MBA are transportable to another organisation, a Japanese organisation may not share your belief.

There are other Master's-level qualifications with very small numbers of participants generally aimed at management specialists of various types. Some universities offer Masters degree courses in Human Resource Management or Industrial Relations, for example.

However, by far the greatest number of people who take a general management qualification in the UK have studied on a Diploma or a Certificate course. In the case of universities, typically the newer ones which were formerly polytechnics, the courses are overseen internally. In other cases, the overseeing is done by an external validating body. Validating bodies include the Business and Technology Education Council (BTEC) in England, Wales and Northern Ireland, the Scottish Vocational Education Council (SCOTVEC) in Scotland, the Open University and the former polytechnics.

The purpose of this validation is to ensure an acceptable standard whenever these qualifications are offered so that employers and participants on the programmes know that anyone with one of these qualifications has acquired a roughly equivalent set of capabilities. The validating bodies are, therefore, watchdogs for the consumers, whether studying in programmes themselves or as employers or potential employers of participants.

Many other private commercial ventures or small-scale institutes offer courses in general management and some of these will give a diploma or certificate. There is a danger with some of these qualifications that they will not be taken seriously by an employer, particularly if the level of study and the effort you have to put in is much lower than a course with an equivalent title. So you should check very carefully the recognition and standing of any course that is not offered by a university or a college of higher or further education. If the course is not recognised, then you need to be sure that you are getting something unique or learning something you can only obtain this way.

Some Diplomas and Certificates in specialist areas of management are offered by professional institutes such as Purchasing, Marketing, and Personnel Management. You need to make sure that any course that you put your time and effort into is nationally recognised and will carry some weight with both employers and academic institutions. Increasingly, Diploma and Certificate courses are being offered which are industry specific, such as a Post Graduate Diploma in Leisure Management. These have a distinct disadvantage (see next paragraph) but the advantage of specialisation and recognition within the industry may outweigh this consideration.

Finally, very large numbers of people going to university or college for the first time study for a degree or diploma in Business Studies. These are offered at a great many academic institutions and are very useful for people entering business or public sector work. They are not, however, aimed at managers and tend to be more broken down into basic academic subjects at the start of the course.

All management programmes expect you to have at least

some work experience and most require you to have held or be about to hold managerial responsibility. On a Business Studies degree course that is not the case. You would therefore find yourself with younger, much less experienced people.

Most people find that one of the greatest benefits in attending a management programme is the opportunity to share experiences with people from different management backgrounds, varying not only in the type of industry but also in professional perspective. Most groups will have managers from the public and the private sectors, from different manufacturing and service organisations, and a range of specialist functions — accountants, personnel managers, marketing managers and production managers.

In summary, therefore, there are three broad levels of general management qualification and at each of these levels some specialised management programmes for people with responsibilities in finance, marketing, systems, personnel, and so on:

- The Certificate in Management or Certificate in Management Studies, generally offered at colleges of higher education and some universities, is aimed at first line managers and supervisors.
- The Diploma in Management Studies, offered at about 70 universities and colleges, and the Diploma in Business Administration, offered at a few universities, are aimed at middle managers mainly with operational responsibilities.
- The Master of Business Administration, or MSc in Management, or similar title, offered in about 60 UK university business or management schools, and in countries all over the world, is aimed primarily at managers who have, or are expected to have, strategic responsibilities and people whose work involves advising managers on strategic matters.

Transferring credits between courses

Until recently, these programmes tended to be quite separate entities provided for particular market segments. Increasingly now it is possible to move between courses and to allow study undertaken on other programmes to count in obtaining a qualification. This allows for the more flexible use of the academic institutions and enables you to build up your own tailor-made programme leading to a qualification or to gain credit for programmes you have already attended.

Where a single institution offers two or even all three levels of qualification, the possession of one may give you the exemption from the first year of the course which follows on. There may however be time limits on the granting of these exemptions. The field of management as a branch of study is a developing one, and the academic bodies are tending to put a 'shelf life' on their own products.

Learning contracts

Quite a number of management programmes now feature the use of a 'learning contract'. This is a variation of the personal development agreement discussed on pages 123–125 of Part II. Instead of involving just you and your boss, the contract is made three ways: between you, your boss and your college tutor.

It allows you to negotiate on the use of the programme and in particular may let you shape the linkages between the programme and your work. For instance, you may be able to establish how newly acquired skills from the programme will be consolidated by opportunities to use them at work and you may be able to have things that you are learning at work acknowledged as part of the programme.

New developments

The impetus of the McCormick/Constable and Handy reports gave rise to a major debate on management education in this country. The main outcome has been a growing recognition of the value of management training, and hence a greater emphasis on the need for qualified managers. Partly as a result of this pressure the provision of courses at all three levels has greatly increased.

The Management Charter Initiative (MCI) has emphasised the provision of training within a qualification hierarchy, and the progression from Certificate to Diploma to Masters is now seen as more natural and desirable. The MCI has also encouraged a move from 'management education' relying heavily on academic knowledge towards 'management training' based on the acquisition of skills and assessment of competences.

The upgrading of polytechnics to universities in 1992 has had several effects on the provision of management training. There has been a shift from external validation by the former Council for National Academic Awards (CNAA) to internal validation. In many cases the new universities (those which were formerly polytechnics) have 'merged' with Colleges of Higher Education, and consequently the hierarchical nature of course provision is becoming more standardised and integrated. This trend also is paralleled in the practice of some institutions franchising others to run their management courses and to validate them locally.

These positive trends of increased provision and standardisation are not solely altruistic. The growing emphasis on financial accountability of tertiary education institutions had already forced them to look to the market place much more explicitly. One consequence is the wider marketing of management courses, particularly to overseas students; their proportion, especially at the Masters level, is increasing steadily.

How might a management qualification affect my job prospects?

First of all, it is important to emphasise that at present formal management qualifications are very rarely required for management jobs despite these changes in provision that have taken place recently.

It is possible that some organisations will require newly appointed managers to undertake a Certificate course. These are likely to be organisations who already provide considerable in-company training for junior managers. In these cases the Certificate programme will be organised through a college by the organisation, and you are not likely to be required to undertake the programme as an individual initiative.

The MBA is, however, sometimes required in some very limited spheres. These are:

- strategic planning and development roles, usually in corporate departments
- corporate financial analysis roles
- work in large management consultancies.

In addition, there is an increasing trend in some large companies to undertake an MBA selection round to increase the supply of people available for promotion to senior management.

For the most part, however, applicants for management jobs are judged on a composite picture of their past achievements, of which one element may well be the extent to which there is evidence of self-development. Therefore, many employers are looking for a much wider range of achievements, one of which might be a management qualification.

Traditional scepticism

There are also, however, some employers who are deeply sceptical of management qualifications, especially the MBA. Surveys have shown that many employers believe that people with MBAs will expect to be paid a lot more than their peers, and are likely to be less inclined to muck in and sort out the day-to-day routine problems that all managers face. These employers also believe that those with MBAs expect to be promoted at an unrealistic rate.

Perceptions of the DMS and the Certificate are not so clear. On the whole, those that know anything about them regard the qualifications well but certainly they are unlikely to expect to pay someone much more who has one of these qualifications.

Perhaps it needs to be borne in mind that the senior managers of today tend to be the middle managers of yesterday who predate formal management training. Very often they are sceptical of something they do not understand, and may even perceive as personally threatening. As today's qualified middle managers progress to senior management, this traditional scepticism should greatly lessen.

Shifting attitudes

However, given the debate which is still taking place and the vast increase in numbers of those obtaining management qualifications, it is likely that employers' perceptions will change and that this will also influence the content and style of management programmes so that employers will increasingly see them as 'more relevant to our needs'.

In judging the value of the qualification to you, you should therefore recognise that the ability to put this achievement on your CV is not going to revolutionise your job prospects at present, except in a very limited number of spheres. However, the picture is changing and the absence of a management qualification could affect your job prospects in some companies especially at the early stages of your career.

At present a qualification is more likely to affect your prospects if it helps you become confident and competent in doing your job and therefore enhances your record of performance and promotion.

So you will need to consider the following questions:

- Will it make any difference to my career, my capability and my motivation whether I have a management qualification or not, particularly if many more people are getting qualified?
- If I want to get a qualification, what is likely to be the best route for me?
- How can I make best use of any existing courses I have attended to get my qualification more easily?

About the main courses

In choosing a course you need to try to assess:

- Is the level and scope of the course right for my capabilities and aspirations?
- Is the style going to match my way of learning and what I need to learn?
- Is the quality going to be up to my standard?

In this section we will, therefore, give more information on the three main course levels, entry qualifications, content, modes, and teaching styles, and give you an indication of what to look for at each level which would help you judge the quality of what is on offer.

Certificate-level programmes

Entry

The Certificate in Management Studies and the Certificate in Management are aimed at first level managers. Some participants may have obtained a degree in, say, Engineering but for the most part, participants will not have any particular qualifications.

Emphasis

The Certificate concentrates on developing usable skills for management rather than just imparting knowledge. It is generally structured in a way that helps individuals to develop themselves. In many cases this will be achieved through having part of the programme devoted to personal effectiveness and also in some cases through the use of 'self-managed learning'.

Content

The programme introduces participants to the main functions of the business and to the day-to-day skills used within them such as budgeting, quality control, and planning work schedules. It also gives very considerable attention to the acquisition of skills in dealing with people. Finally it addresses the immediate environment of the organisation,

looking at customers and markets, economic and technological factors, and so on.

These programmes are mainly offered on a one-year part-
time basis but in some cases they are 13-week full-time
programmes which may be sponsored by a company as part
of their management training scheme. One of the particular
benefits of the part-time version is the very wide range of
participants it attracts and, therefore, the opportunities for
learning from people with different backgrounds.

The CMS is, therefore, a good course of study for you if:

- You have just become or are expecting to become a
  manager and want to acquire some relevant skills and
  overall understanding of the organisation and its context.
- You have not studied for many years and want to get back
  into education with other people like yourself.

You can find out more about these programmes from BTEC
and SCOTVEC and from local colleges and universities.

Diploma in Management Studies (DMS)

Entry

Although this is described as a post-graduate qualification,
many institutions are very flexible about accepting mature
managers without qualifications onto the programme
provided that they have the right level of work experience.
Having a CMS would undoubtedly be an acceptable entry
qualification in most cases.

This home-grown UK qualification is aimed at middle level
operational managers and is offered in over 70 universities and
colleges. In some of these there is a link with an MBA
programme where the DMS forms the earlier part of the course
of study.

DMS programmes tend to follow a fairly standardised
pattern and it is therefore possible to transfer to a programme
at another college if you change jobs. Participants tend to be in
their late twenties and early thirties and will generally include
a good mixture of experience from public and private sector

and from all management functions. In some colleges, public sector and private sector participants are separated into different versions of the programme.

Content

The DMS generally gives a good understanding of how the business works and what skills, techniques, and understanding can be used at operational levels to make the organisation as effective as possible. The shape of these programmes has varied very little over the last 25 years and they tend to be arranged in three parts. In the first, subjects studied provide background in economics, organisational behaviour, quantitative methods, accounting, and so on. In the second, the emphasis shifts to more applied topics such as marketing, information systems, human resource manage-ment, and financial management. The third part is generally intended to bring the bits together and will usually involve some consideration of business strategy and require the participant to undertake a work-based project with recommendations for action.

The DMS will have more assessments than a CMS although many of these will not be the conventional three-hour exam.

The majority of DMS participants study on a part-time basis, when it is normally a two-year period of study. Many Diploma-level programmes are under review at present because the advent of the MBA in greater numbers requires colleges to review how the programmes should differ from one another and what linkages should exist between them.

The DMS is a good course of study for you if:

- You work for a supportive organisation that is prepared to give you time off work for study and/or practical help to enable you to complete the course.
- You have until recently been working in a professional, technical or functional area and are now undertaking managerial duties that increasingly bring you into contact with other departments and that give you a real responsibility for the performance of a department.
- You have been a line manager for some years and are now responsible for quite a large number of people.

- You have the confidence and persistence to undertake a sustained course of study at high level.

Master of Business Administration (MBA)

The MBA is mainly aimed at those who have, or are expected to have, strategic responsibilities in an organisation. Emphasis tends to be placed on analysing the business and its issues from the perspective of senior management.

Entry

In most MBA programmes you are expected to have a degree or professional qualification and at least five years' work experience to enter the programme. There are, however, variations and these are likely to affect the composition of the groups on the programme.

There are a small number of two-year MBA programmes and these tend to allow shorter levels of work experience for very bright entrants. They therefore are likely to attract younger participants. A consequence of this is that there is relatively more emphasis on the 'knowledge' of the faculty, and the use of the participant's own experience is less important.

On the whole one-year full-time MBA programmes, which are only offered in universities, tend to have an older composition because of the experience requirements for those courses. However, they tend to insist on a degree or professional qualification although there are some that will use the Graduate Management Admission Test (GMAT) which is a 3½-hour aptitude test designed to measure certain mental capabilities considered important to the study of management at the graduate level. It is an American test used extensively in the United States and elsewhere.

Many of the UK university business and management schools offer Masters degrees on a part-time basis. On the whole, entry qualifications are more flexible for part-time degrees, the expectation being that work experience is relatively more important.

New types of MBA

Several MBA degrees are offered on a distance learning basis backed up by occasional attendance and there are a number with modular structure of intensive periods of study interspersed with time back at work. Recent developments include the 'closed' MBA programme run for managers drawn from only one sponsoring organisation and the Consortium MBA, where a group of organisations work with a particular academic institution and sponsor participants onto a specially designed MBA programme that may include project work within the company.

Depending upon these variations in entry qualification and length, the programmes tend to attract different types of applicant and to emphasise different features.

Content

All MBA programmes call for extremely hard work and cover a very wide variety of subjects in considerably more depth than the generalist would need. Undertaking an MBA is therefore a major commitment that will have an effect not just on your job, but also on your private life. Bear in mind that your commitment is likely to spread over the period from September to June with little respite at Christmas or Easter.

You can expect an MBA programme to cover finance, marketing, operations, business strategy, quantitative methods and computing, organisational behaviour, in depth, and often with more than one course in each subject. This depth of coverage of each of these subjects should be sufficient for you to enter this field of work.

MBA programmes are normally modular in design. Typically you will have to undertake a large number of core modules but, especially in the second and third years, you will have the opportunity to take non-core modules as electives. Elective modules are generally offered 'subject to there being sufficient numbers' and so it is a good idea to find out which electives are regularly run and which only run occasionally. If you have a particular selection of electives in mind, check that such a combination will be possible, as electives are often timetabled simultaneously.

There is likely to be a heavier load of assessment than in any other management course. So find out what the assessments for the course are and consider whether you can manage this quantity of work.

You will also be expected to undertake a major project or dissertation which makes significant recommendations to the senior management of the organisation, affecting its strategic direction. If it is a full-time programme you will be given help in finding a suitable project. However, if it is a part-time programme, you will be expected to have appropriate level project work in your own organisation. If you are not in a position to undertake a project of a sufficiently strategic level, then you may be unable to pass this part of the programme.

Methods

One further point to look at in MBA programmes is the extent to which they emphasise case study methods. This method uses material from real business situations as a basis for analysis and discussion to identify the problems facing that company. It is valuable as a way of highlighting the complexity of these situations and for developing different strategies for dealing with them. However, it is often criticised for being abstract and for requiring recommendations for solving problems, stopping short of the difficult process of implementing these recommendations. You may wish to discover how much emphasis is placed on case studies and the development of analytical skills and how much this is balanced by other methods.

An MBA programme is a good course of study if:

- You are at the beginning of your career, did well at university, studied a subject that you can't or don't want to make immediate use of and want to get into business in one of the following areas – marketing, business planning, or corporate finance.
- You have had several years' experience in an industry or a profession that you now wish to leave completely for a management career elsewhere.

- You have had several years in a functional management role and now want to be involved in general management at a strategic level.
- You want to pursue a career in a financial institution in the city or in consultancy.
- You are able to devote a major share of your time and energy to it, probably over two to three years for a part-time programme.

To find out more about DMS and MBA courses contact your local university and/or college. Your local library will normally have some information on file, and will probably have some of the directories of courses which are published commercially. AMBA, the Association of MBAs, publishes a useful guide.

The way in which courses differ

1. Modes of study
Many universities and colleges try to offer their courses with patterns of attendance that will suit the needs of working managers. So most of the qualifications that have been described are offered on a full-time and a part-time basis. They may also be offered in a block release or sandwich mode. A few qualifications are also offered on a distance learning basis where the need to attend college is brought down to about one study week a year.

Here are some points, therefore, for you to consider about the various modes of study.

Full-time For many people this is an impractical way of studying; their employer is unlikely to give them leave to be away from work for large chunks of the year. Even if the employer would give leave, people often feel that there are too many strings attached to the offer and worry that they may be cutting themselves off from what is going on at work.

However, full-time study may be best for you if:

- you are making a real change of career direction, for instance from accountancy to business management, or from public sector manager to private sector manager.
- you want a total immersion in an experience which will help you make a fundamental change of direction.
- you want to explore a range of subjects in great depth and are looking for intellectual enrichment and challenge.

Obviously the financial impact of a full-time course is enormous if you are paying for it yourself. Later on in this section we will look at how to assess the value of such an investment to you.

Part-time This can include a number of different patterns of attendance, many of which require you to take some time away from work. If your employer will support you to attend during work hours, then you will need to consider with your immediate boss how your work will be covered in your absence and what effect it will have on you and on the work.

It is likely that an employer will take more seriously a course that causes you to be away during working hours. You will get more comment and teasing, people will have higher expectations, but you can also expect more interest in what you are doing and perhaps some practical support.

Some of the more imaginative patterns of part-time study include those which put the bulk of attendance either into evenings or weekends but also have one or two weeks of intensive full-time study during the year.

Sandwich This mode of study is generally only offered on courses where it is expected that the participants are at the start of their career. You are therefore not likely to find it in management courses.

Block Release or Modular Attendance

A very small number of MBA and DMS programmes are offered on the basis of periods of full-time study, perhaps for four weeks at a time, with projects to undertake during the time back at work. Consider such programmes if:

- you want to get the intensity of full-time study but can't get a whole year off work.
- you would prefer to get away from home for periods of study and then lead a more normal family life in between times rather than being a pain-in-the-neck for a whole year or more.

Distance Learning Modes

Since the foundation of the Open University (OU), distance learning has become a widely used form of study. Now many other colleges and universities run programmes in this mode, where they send the learning materials to you rather than you attending regular classes. In some cases, such as the OU, tutorial support is provided locally.

Courses run in this way can provide you with a very convenient way of studying. They allow you to study at a time that suits you. In most cases they also make it possible for you to spread the courses out over a longer period than would be possible in a conventional qualification programme.

Some people learn better when they can pace the work to suit themselves and they may feel more able to concentrate and absorb information studying alone. But you must consider very carefully the following points:

- Some of the best experiences on management programmes come from sharing information and ideas with other managers from very different backgrounds. In distance learning you are on your own most of the time. You will have very little chance of discussion and are likely to feel isolated

- It may become hard for you to maintain the self-discipline to study regularly if there is no social pressure to attend, or time structure provided, or attractions of meeting other people.
- Some of the inspiration in a good course comes from the ability of the teacher or tutor to make you enthusiastic about the subject and its relevance. For courses with no tutorial support you will have to get that entirely from the subject and the written material provided.

For these reasons many of the distance learning programmes provide for some periods of study together. During these periods, of course, it is possible to concentrate exclusively on those areas where you learn best as a group and not waste the time of the group on activities which are probably best learned individually, such as computer packages and knowledge-based learning which is best acquired through reading.

A particular feature of the Open University courses is that they have open entry. In other words, you do not have to normal university entry qualifications to undertake the course. This open entry applies to many distance learning courses.

These programmes often place great emphasis on work-based projects and assignments so they may be seen as more relevant to the work situation as well as more convenient. These features, together with the perception that you have to be really committed and make considerable personal sacrifice to undertake the course successfully, have tended to make employers very supportive of distance learning modes of study.

Ideally, therefore, if you do not have the time to attend a conventional course, choose some of these mixed programmes with an emphasis on distance learning. However, you can make a programme with almost exclusively distance learning work for you if:

- You have no alternative – you are living in the Outer Hebrides or you work evenings in a town where the only appropriate course is offered evenings only, *and* you are a highly self-disciplined person.
- You can get a group around you. These could be people you don't know that the university or college puts you in touch with or they could be people you persuade to study with you. If there are enough of you, you could even occasionally share the cost of a tutor to work with you.

Open Learning Modes

Open learning applies not only to the open entry which exists on most courses described in this way, but also to their openness to adaptation to meet your needs.

A small number of courses of this type exist, but the philosophy is present, to some extent, in a larger number of programmes. You are able to negotiate how you will learn (in terms of timescales and ways of studying or learning) and also what you will learn. This can allow you to bring together unusual groups of subject areas as well as letting you take charge over the pace and style of learning.

2. Style of course

Quite a number of factors will affect the style of the course in ways that will make it more or less suitable to your needs.

For instance, if you have a good degree in, say, economics, and five years' working experience including some management, it may be tempting to go to a programme that is full of people just like you, which emphasises intellectual rigour and brings you into contact with brilliant faculty who do world-wide high-level consulting. But you should also be thinking about balancing up the areas where you may be relatively less strong and consider which course will deepen your interpersonal skills, give you a lot of insight into implementing change, sharpen your capability in day-to-day financial control, or develop your understanding of customers and their needs. It may therefore be best for you to attend a programme where the other participants are not quite so high-powered but who represent scores of years of experience in a wide variety of industries and functions. You may also need to consider the balance between skills-based and knowledge-based learning.

Making a judgement – don't be fooled by glossy hype

Of course it is quite difficult to judge these features from the outside. But by reading brochures in a discerning way and questioning the course leader at the academic institution you can get quite a good picture. In a brochure, you will find that the knowledge-based and more cerebral/intellectual content tends to be described as 'analytical', 'rigorous', 'broadening', and 'stimulating'. It may say that the course will lead to 'questioning' and 'objective' approaches. For the skills- and competence-based content, the words to look for are 'applied', 'project', 'relevant', 'focused', and sometimes 'student-centred'.

You may also find that the emphasis of the course is reflected in the teaching staff. In the more knowledge-based programmes, teaching staff will often be described in terms of the research they have done.

In the programmes that tend to lead into consultancy jobs and the financial institutions, teaching staff are usually much involved in consulting at high levels themselves.

Warning signs

Danger signals are, therefore, where the course claims to be of a particular type, but the information about the faculty makes this look impossible. For instance, a programme that is for operational managers at middle levels is unlikely to be much good if none of the faculty has recent experience in managing operations themselves or undertaking extensive consultancy at operational levels.

Pacing

One final feature you may wish to consider is the pace and intensity of the programme. This is, of course, to some extent determined by the mode of study. But different courses tend to generate very different degrees of intensity by the way they are structured and the atmosphere created by the staff. The most reliable way of judging this feature and most other factors related to style is to make the opportunity to meet people who have attended the same course recently. It will depend on your life style, what you are looking for, and on your learning preferences, whether you want gradual drip feed and slow assimilation or an intense, demanding, but transformational experience.

3. Subject content and emphasis

In many courses, there may be a bias either toward quantitative subjects or toward the 'softer' subjects such as organisational behaviour and the management of change. Some have a balance between the two. You may, therefore, want to consider the content of the programme and the background and interests of the faculty to help you decide which areas you will have strengthened by attending this programme.

Don't just play to your strengths

Some people are tempted to continue to go over ground that they have found easy at other times. Thus you find people who have strong numerate skills undertaking a professional accountancy qualification and later going on to do an MBA where they specialise in financial subjects. Meanwhile back at work they may be weak in those areas that require them to consider customers or the workforce and may therefore make a limited contribution to the business. Furthermore they may never get beyond the number two position in a department because of their narrow focus.

4. Costs

The cost of qualification courses in management varies considerably so you will have to check up on the current fee level and find out what changes there are likely to be during your programme.

In general, the following can be said about costs:

- At present, management education in the UK, including MBA programmes, tends to be cheap relative to, say, France and the USA.
- Undergraduate programmes will remain cheaper because they are subsidised by the state.
- Universities tend to be more expensive than colleges.

Assessing the quality of a programme

Apart from all the factors mentioned above, some courses are just better than others. The factors that make a course good all revolve around the capability and commitment of the course team – the staff who run the programme — and the quality and variety of backgrounds of course members.

Before attending the programme you therefore need to assure yourself that the quality of the staff will be worth the effort you are going to have to put in.

You can do this by assessing the following:

- How up-to-date are the staff? Are they still learning?
- How good are they at getting people to learn in a challenging but enjoyable way?
- How well organised are they? Do things happen on time? Are the right documents available? Can you find them when you need them?
- How flexible are they in responding to the needs of different participants?
- How recently has the course been reviewed and modified to meet changing customer requirements?

You can get a lot of information before attending by doing the following:

- Ensure that you are interviewed and make sure it is a two-way discussion.
- Ask what work staff do or have done recently outside the college or university.
- Ask for details of reading, assessments, course schemes, and so on, and see how well prepared they are.
- Get the names and phone numbers of at least two people currently or recently on the course and ask them about the quality of the staff and fellow students – in particular, ask them about the enthusiasm of the course team for their work on the programme.
- Ask if you can attend a session in the current programme.
- Find out if students have published an 'alternative' prospectus that provides a consumer's view of the course.

In all of these, you are looking for evidence of the staff's academic standing, management experience, openness to change and growth, and responsiveness to participants' needs. Questions to be asked might be:

- What feedback mechanisms do staff use to assess how effective they and the programme are?
- How have the content and structure of the programme changed over the years? – in some cases you will find they have just bolted on new subjects; in others that they

have genuinely modified the programme to match changes in the manager's job.

- Do you get a sense that they are concerned for you to develop a capacity to manage your own learning more effectively as a result of the programme and for you to gain real insight into the process of managing, or is it just a series of topics and techniques?
- Do you feel confident that your performance as a manager will be enhanced by being in contact with these staff and students in completing the programme?

Getting the best out of a management programme

A simple rule of thumb tends to be 'the more you put in, the more you get out'.

While you are on a programme, you are in touch with a wealth of useful contacts, information and learning opportunities. So, if you just do the minimum to scrape by in your assessments, you are unlikely to learn anything like as much as those who enthusiastically grab every opportunity they can. The work load in some of these programmes is very heavy and it may therefore be tempting to cut yourself off from other people, get a wet towel round your head and get on with it. However, some of the most successful participants team up with one or more other course members to chew over what they are learning, share information and books, discuss one another's work and talk through problems.

A management programme, especially one where you are away from people in your own organisation, is a great place to experiment, take risks and even make a complete fool of yourself. It also offers a wonderful opportunity to review where you are and where you are going.

These programmes often get a bad reputation with employers because people who go on them not only come back with new and challenging ideas but also are more likely to seek new job opportunities and decide to make a change. If you've got a miserable employer, you may want to assess the options and change jobs. If your employer is supportive, this is an opportunity to be seen in a new light.

Most programmes require you to do some practical, work-based projects. For your employer, it may be the possibility of getting some free consultancy. Try to get something significant to do which will bring you into contact with interesting people and maybe raise your own political awareness as well as your profile. If you choose your topic carefully, you may be able to have as your tutor someone who can really help your development as well as helping your organisation.

At a deeper level, however, attending a long-term educational programme can have some really good pay-offs in terms of self-confidence and understanding yourself a good deal better. In order to get these pay-offs, it is essential to enter into the programme with an open mind, aware that there are many things you don't know. Those who spend their time trying to prove to the others in the programme how clever they are and how much they already know, rarely learn very much at all.

Finally, it is important to keep giving attention to the link between learning and doing throughout the programme. This means wherever possible exploring the possibilities of implementing your learning at work as soon after the programme as you can and reviewing what you have learned in the light of the practical realities of your organisation. This process can give rise to some real discomfort and disharmony – people reject you, you create confusion because your ideas don't fit, or you realise you have an awful lot to learn. But that's it – real learning is often painful. So get stuck in – use everything that happens to add to your experience.

The evaluation

You are a customer. You are deciding whether to buy a product. You might be paying yourself or you may be buying on behalf of your organisation, which is paying. You want to be as sure as possible that you are going to get good value for the time and money spent. This is therefore an investment decision.

● *What will attending the programme cost?*
Of course this first depends on whether you do it full-time or
part-time and what the fees are, but don't forget all the other
costs that you will incur: some of these are not financial – for
instance they might relate to relationships which will be
affected.

● *Will the experience be worthwhile in its own right?*
This will depend on:
● How appropriate the programme is for you at this stage in
  your life.
● How good the quality of the programme is.
● How much you are prepared to put in.

● *How valuable will the learning from the programme and the
  qualification be?*
This will be mainly reflected in how much of what you learned
can be used to make work more interesting, your performance
better, your prospects of promotion greater and, most
important of all, your understanding of yourself deeper.
These are the real reasons for buying the 'product'. You might
also be lucky and find that the qualification adds to your
earning capacity. Quite often it doesn't but if it does that's a
great bonus.

Management short courses

If the range of what is on offer in management qualification
courses is large, the range in management short courses is
even larger. This is, of course, the sphere in which commercial
organisations, as well as the universities and colleges,
operate. There is no control whatsoever in this area – anybody
can book a hotel room, advertise a course and take the money
from the customers.

There are really excellent short courses and there is trash:
there is also everything between the two extremes.

Much of what we have said about qualification courses can
be applied to short courses, but you may feel that it is not

worth your while to undertake too much of an investigation for a course which is only going to take up say three days of your time.

However, do put in the effort. All worthwhile providers will agree to give you the name of previous customers if the course has run before. But in this sphere, many valuable short courses run on a one-off basis because the topic is new and of contemporary relevance. Some subjects are so specialised that they are only covered in short courses.

So get advice, preferably from more than one person, not only on what is available, but also how good it is.

Structuring the decision

To help you go about making the right choice, here is a check list of the factors to take into consideration:

- **Your background**
  What qualifications do you already hold?
  How much managerial experience do you already have?
- **Your plans**
  Do you need a qualification to help you reach a career goal?
  Do you want to specialise to broaden your knowledge and experience?
- **Your commitment**
  Can you undertake a full-time course or a part-time course?
  Are your family prepared to share your commitment?
- **The right level**
  Are you choosing a level that is neither too difficult nor too easy?
  Are you going to enter at a level that will allow further development?
- **The right format**
  Are you choosing a course which has a delivery format that is best suited to you?
  Are you choosing a course that allows you to use the learning styles which suit you best?

- **The costs**
  Are you or your company going to pay the tuition fees?
  Are you or your company going to pay the costs of text books, travelling etc?
- **The immediate future**
  Will you be in a position to see the chosen course through to the end? If not, will you be able to transfer to another institution midstream?

A final cautionary note

The MBA in particular has been described as a 'passport to dissatisfaction', but this description could also be applied to other management qualifications. If dissatisfaction does arise, it is usually the result of either false expectations or frustration with your bosses and the company you work for.

The most common false expectations are automatic promotion and a pay rise. Neither can be expected to come as of right from gaining a management qualification. In any case, it is only sensible to discuss with your boss what your expectations might reasonably be, before you start a particular course.

One MBA participant has described his course as 'a year of realising how ignorant I was, followed by two years of realising how ignorant my bosses were.' It is much harder to predict or to overcome this kind of frustration. It may be indicative of the fact that you need to look elsewhere to develop your career.

Our final advice then is to see a management qualification as an investment in yourself and your career rather than as an investment in your present job.

Good luck!

Part IV Glossary of Management Development Terms

Glossary of Management Development Terms

Accreditation of Prior Learning (APL) is a formalised system for equating previous study or, increasingly, previous work experience with elements of course work in order to grant exemptions. In the latter case, difficult decisions have to be made about the quality as well as the quantity of experience. Exemption from doing a module of a course is often granted but exemption from assessment of that module is not.

Action-centred Leadership is a training approach to leadership which concentrates on fulfilling three main needs in a team: (i) that the task objectives are met, (ii) that team spirit and co-operation are maintained, and (iii) that the personal needs of each individual are allowed for and met.

Action Learning involves groups of managers being brought together to solve actual organisational problems, and to learn through that process, as opposed to solving theoretical problems in an artificial environment. An adviser encourages members of the group to share experience, question one another, give feedback and tease out generally applicable learning. The group also encourages commitment to action and follow-up and review. Action learning may involve bringing in 'experts' when the group needs their contribution for the resolution of a task.

Assertiveness Training aims to enable people to convey legitimate needs or grievances to others without feeling embarrassed or guilty for causing offence. The assertiveness takes the form of honesty, not aggression.

Assessment Centre is a term used to describe a series of simulated managerial situations to which candidates for promotion to management positions are submitted as part of a process of evaluation and selection. The assessment period can last several days, during which the behaviour of the participants is observed by managers trained to assess performance against predetermined 'dimensions', such as problem analysis, judgement, and persuasiveness. Situations used include In-basket Exercise (qv), Leaderless Group Discussions (qv), planning exercises, and interviews with the observers. In addition, psychological test batteries may be applied.

Biography work involves individuals examining their life history to date (including education, talents, career pattern, family situation, etc), with the aim of reaching a better understanding of strengths, weaknesses, behaviour patterns, etc. The understanding can then be used as a basis for future planning. The method can include group discussion, lectures, and individual questioning.

Brainstorming, a form of Creativity Training (qv), is a creative group problem-solving exercise in which members are encouraged to express any ideas leading to a solution, however far-fetched, which spring to mind. The emphasis is on positive contribution; members are discouraged from passing judgement on any of the suggestions thrown up.

BTEC Business and Technology Education Council, which is the central monitoring body for Higher National Diplomas and some other qualifications.

Business Game A training exercise involving two or more teams, representing typical but simplified businesses, competing over a greatly compressed time-span. Team members are given specific roles within a company, and must take decisions on company operations based on given information. Feedback is provided on each decision in terms of its effect on the performance of the company. The aim is to survive, and preferably to do better than the competition on certain measurable criteria, usually financial.

Career Life Planning A form of career development which helps managers identify their career goals, abilities, and level of motivation. Having thus achieved a greater level of self-awareness, they can then map out more realistic future career plans, and should be able to exercise greater control over their career development in the light of those plans.

Case Study Method A problem-solving exercise which involves the presentation of a realistic problem situation within an organisation (real or imaginary), for which possible solutions can then be explored in group discussion. The case study can be presented in written form or on film, and may vary in complexity and detail. It is often pre-issued, either before a class meeting in which it is discussed in syndicate or prior to a written exam.

Coaching is the process by which a someone helps colleagues improve their approach to solving problems or accomplishing a task. The coach and the colleague work jointly through a problem or a task challenge which has been selected for its learning potential. Afterwards they review and evaluate the outcome in order to draw out the important learning implications for both of them. Plans can then be made to apply the lessons learned in fresh situations.

Co-counselling (Re-evaluation Counselling, Reciprocal Counselling, Peer Counselling, Exchange Counselling) An exercise in personal development involving two people who take it in turns to be client and counsellor. The counsellor's role is a supportive one, in which clients are encouraged to re-examine and gain greater insight into their pasts, and to free themselves from any restrictive, negative attitudes and beliefs.

Computer-Assisted Learning (Computer-Assisted Instruction) A method of learning which uses the computer either as a learning resource or as a positive teaching medium. In the first instance, the learner accesses, for example, simulations, or problem-solving exercises on the computer. In the second, the presentation of the instructional material is adapted to the capability of the learner by the computer, based on that learner's responses.

Consciousness-Raising Group Through group discussion and sharing of personal experience, a consciousness-raising group aims to discover to what extent experiences and problems are purely personal, and to what extent they are imposed by society. In the latter instance, a group may then decide to take positive political action to bring about improvements in the social structure, eg equal rights for women in management.

Consortium The term is used in management development in two ways. There is a consortium of companies that come together to provide a particular programme over which they have some or complete control. There is also a consortium of academic institutions that club together to be able to provide a wider range of services to clients.

Continuing Professional Development (CPD) is now a requirement of some professional institutes for more experienced members, with a view to keeping them up to date through attending a required number of short courses. It may include some management development.

Creativity Training takes as its premise the belief that everyone has a creative capacity: it merely needs to be stimulated and developed. This is done by a variety of different training techniques which encourage new, imaginative, and unusual ways of thinking and problem-solving. (See also: Brainstorming, Lateral Thinking, Synectics.)

Credit Accumulation and *Credit Transfer* are based on the notion that a qualification can be obtained from more than one academic or other institution. Credit transfer allows you to use a course that you have completed elsewhere to count toward a qualification in a particular institution. In credit accumulation, you can build up a series of credits so that they can be seen as equivalent to a particular qualification or level of development. The credits can be obtained for work experience, in-company or other training programmes, projects, and parts of qualification courses. Credit accumulation requires some body or some institution to agree standards and say what activities are equivalent.

Critical Incident Analysis involves using the description of one or more critical incidents which have taken place within a manager's organisation. Analysis of the features of the incident(s) is used to learn both from successes and from failures or near-failures. It can be a group method, or can be used individually with a manager or developer.

Development Centre is used for programmes similar to that of an Assessment Centre (qv), but here the evaluation of participants is not used for selection purposes but solely as a basis for deciding their developmental needs and starting to make plans to meet those needs.

Diary Exercise Participants in this training exercise record their daily work activities in a diary over a 10- to 14-day period. The entries are then reviewed, either one-to-one with a boss, or in a group, to assess how time is being spent, what is being demanded of the manager, and whether any improvements can be made in approach and time allocation. The diary exercises may be associated with analysis of training/development needs, awareness raising, or structural change.

Directed Private Study A method of tuition involving a mixture of face-to-face and correspondence tuition. A typical pattern would be: (i) an initial intensive class session; (ii) a long period of correspondence learning; (iii) a second period of class tuition, possibly culminating in exams.

Distance Learning (Distance Teaching, Teaching at a Distance) A form of Programmed Learning (qv) carried out through written/audio and video materials, or, more recently, computer conferencing, eg the Open University. The materials may prescribe a schedule of knowledge to be absorbed, and may also encourage an interactive process of questioning, information collection and review.

Experiential Learning is learning through doing. Typically, it involves an exercise such as a simulation, an outdoor activity or a 'game'. These are used as vehicles for testing out ideas, theories and particular aspects of behaviour. The exercise is followed by some form of structured discussion and reflection with a view to extracting lessons from the experience.

Flexistudy A learning system which combines home study with occasional college-based tutorials and seminars. Some of the flexibility may relate to times of attendance. Others relate to the type of learning preferred.

GMAT Graduate Management Admission Test, known at one time as the Princeton Test. It is a 3½-hour aptitude test used widely in American business schools to measure certain mental capabilities considered important to the study of management at the graduate level.

Handout Information given (usually) as a complement to a lecture. A handout may: provide background information which is developed in the lecture; outline the objectives of the lecture; summarise the main points; present questions/ discussion points; and/or list recommended reading material related to the lecture.

Human Resource Management (HRM) is one of the functions undertaken to some extent in any organisation, private or public, but not always described as such. Employees are seen as a unique resource, an asset to be managed well, invested in and developed — not a liability whose costs must be minimised. In those organisations professing to practice HRM it has taken over the function of Personnel Management. HRM is often perceived as having a much broader remit, related to an organisation's overall strategy, and being more proactive. Management development is likely to be a central part of a comprehensive approach to HRM, involving the effective integration of the needs of the organisation and the individual manager within a planned programme of development.

In-Basket Exercise (In-Tray Exercise) An exercise in which each learner is given the typical contents of a manager's in-tray, all of which require some decision, and a set time in which to deal with the various items. Each learner works alone, but at the end of the allotted time, the items are discussed by the whole class and the optimum action for each one decided upon. In-basket exercises are also frequently used in Assessment Centre (qv) programmes.

Independent Study (Independent Learning, Autonomous Learning) A form of learning in which the influence of the tutor, or the institution, is minimised. The student retains total control over the learning process and major decisions within that process.

Interactive Skills Training Training in the skills used to achieve objectives in face-to-face working contexts. It normally involves active exercises using the necessary skills with feedback from tutors, other participants, and perhaps closed-circuit television.

Inventories Questionnaires about managerial behaviour, thinking processes, values, and organisational features which allow those completing them to make comparisons with others. They can be directed at individual managers, groups, or whole organisations. They are based on subjective perception, not objective measurement, but provide a device for clarifying thinking, developing a common language for discussion, and diagnosing problem areas.

Job Enrichment The redesigning of a job to make it more satisfying and challenging for the employee. This might involve giving greater responsibility for deciding how tasks should be accomplished, for the quality of outputs, etc.

Joint Development Activities Management development projects which take place within a company, organised jointly by its senior managers and a team from an educational institution. The managers work on an actual problem within the organisation, with support and guidance from this combined group.

Lateral Thinking A way of thinking which rejects traditional, rational, logical methods, and uses instead seemingly illogical processes. In order to think laterally, it is necessary to:
- Recognise and reject old ideas which are no longer relevant.
- Seek out many different viewpoints.
- Relax rigid control of thought.
- Allow for the intervention of chance.

In lateral thinking, everything is possible; it is not necessary to be correct all the time. Lateral thinking is a technique used in Creativity Training (qv). (*See also*: Brainstorming, Synectics.)

Leaderless Group Discussion A learning method in which a group of participants are brought together to discuss one or more work-related topics, within a given time-limit. No leader is appointed and no structure given to the discussion beforehand. One or more leaders therefore naturally emerge to take charge of the direction of the discussion. If it is part of an Assessment Centre (qv) programme, assessors are present, but take no active part; they rate the performance of each participant.

Learning Community (Peer Learning Community) A learning situation in which a group of people come together in an environment of openness and trust to meet particular learning needs, and in which they share resources and skills. Each member is responsible both for meeting personal learning needs and for helping the other members to meet theirs.

Learning Contract (Contract Learning, Individual Development Contract) A contract specifying what is to be learnt and how, over what time period, and the criteria on which the learning will be assessed. Usually the contract is a personal one, drawn up jointly between the manager and a person representing the employer or a tutor, to suit the individual's needs and strengths. (*See also*: Personal Development Agreements.)

Learning Organisation (or learning company) is the term used to describe an ideal form of organisation in which the learning of all of its members is facilitated so that the organisation can be continuously transformed. All aspects of the organisation are designed to this end — the approach to strategy and policy formulation; accounting and other control systems; structures of jobs, relationships and rules; and culture. The personal development of individuals is enhanced and the organisation benefits through improved knowledge and information. The overall aim is to increase competitive advantage.

Manager Audit Assessment of the total managerial activity within an organisation, which may be carried out by an internal or an external auditor. It is usually based on a checklist incorporating previously agreed criteria. These criteria may relate to objective characteristics such as age, educational qualifications, and types of experience. They may also relate to assessments which can either be generated from judgements of performance by senior managers or from tests of various types.

Managerial Grid Training A managerial grid is a chart on which managerial style can be rated. One axis represents managers' concern for satisfactory task completion, and the other axis their concern for the people who work for them. The grid is used to identify the manager's preferred management style (expressed by a joint measure of the extent of the concern shown on the two dimensions) and to compare this with the 'ideal' for a particular situation. The aim is generally to increase managers' versatility in the styles they can use and to enhance their understanding of the impact of their style on a variety of contexts.

Mentoring involves one person helping colleagues work through important stages in their development as managers within the context of a complete life and career. While Coaching (qv) focuses on questions of 'how' problems are solved or tasks accomplished, mentoring explores questions of purpose and motivation. This is done by asking 'why' the colleague is behaving in a certain way in relation, for example, to some important transition or challenge at work or in life more generally. The term is also applied to the provision of in-company support to a junior colleague undertaking distance learning.

Module A self-contained and complete unit of knowledge, designed to be assimilated by the learner within a short time-span. The term is often used for a self-contained component of a more extensive training programme or course. A 'modular degree' is one where the student can pick from a series of self-contained units and may study at more than one institution. There is little attempt by the provider to integrate the different parts into some coherent whole, although some restriction of choice may be imposed by specifying some modules as prerequisites for undertaking others.

Motivation Training A group training method in which members are encouraged to set themselves high goals and to develop their need to achieve. The training takes place in a retreat setting, and through a mixture of self-examination and group support, members learn how to improve their effectiveness in achieving set goals, and reinforce their drive to achieve.

Open Learning is a general term conveying freedom for students to pace their own progress through a course of training. It may allow the learner to control pace of learning, the methods (attendance, reading, tutorials, projects), and content of the programme. Open learning courses are usually based on Distance Learning methods (qv).

Organisational Development (OD) is a systematic process which recognises that, collectively, members of an organisation need continuously to reassess its performance so that they and the organisation can learn and develop. To stimulate improvement a wide range of interventions is used many of which involve training and development, especially of managers.

Organisational Role Analysis is carried out by a consultant, and helps managers to define their perceptions of their role within the company, thus helping them to decide how to make any changes necessary for the fulfilment of that role.

Outdoor Training is carried out on intensive residential courses, where small groups of participants engage in a series of tough outdoor tasks demanding group cohesion, strong leadership and skills in managing people. The exercises are totally absorbing and physically strenuous, and aim to develop self-awareness, confidence, self-reliance, as well as group interaction skills. The extent to which outdoor training is relevant to management development or team development depends entirely upon the way in which participants are led to understand the underlying processes in themselves and the team and its connection to the work context.

Performance Review (Performance Appraisal) This usually takes place in a boss-employee interview or discussion, when the employee's performance is evaluated against agreed task objectives, and any necessary changes are discussed. (Considerably more detail on performance reviews is given in Part II of this book.) Systems vary considerably in terms of their formality and bureaucracy, their concentration on past and present performance and future potential, and their relative emphasis on reward or development.

Personal Development Agreements, described in detail in Part II, define explicit understanding about individuals' learning goals and how these might be met within the organisational context. Unlike the Learning Contract (qv) made between students and their tutors personal development agreements are arrived at between employees and their managers acting on behalf of the organisation.

Process Analysis (Behaviour Analysis) involves reviewing and describing the ways in which people are behaving and their effect on the activities of other people. It is normally undertaken as commentary on tasks or discussions in pairs or small groups and the analysis is done by someone not participating in the main activity. Process analysis is usually based on some agreed framework for categorising behaviour. A process consultant is, therefore, a person who is expert in providing feedback on process, and helping to adapt process so that it results in the desired outcomes.

Programmed Learning (Automated Teaching, Individualised Programme Instruction) A self-teaching method, in which the material to be learnt is organised into a programme, or graded sequence of steps, with direct feedback on learner performance given at the end of each step. The learner can progress through these steps at a suitable pace.

Project, Assignment, or Dissertation are terms used almost interchangeably for a finite practical activity of investigation and analysis which usually results in a report with conclusions and recommendations for action. It may be part of an educational or training programme or a free-standing development activity in its own right.

Project Method A learning method involving individual or group investigation of information in a specific subject area, which encourages originality and initiative-taking. Each project culminates in an end-product, such as a report, or a computer program.

Reflective Learning Learning by thinking over and drawing conclusions from immediate or past experience. Computers can help the reflective process by providing feedback on the pattern of the learner's reflections. More commonly reflective learning involves the learner reviewing past experience within some sort of framework for categorising actions, thoughts and feelings. It may involve another person as a questioner.

Resource Centre (Multi-media Study Centre, Learning Resource Centre) A library of a wide range of individual study materials – books, pamphlets, videos, tapes, computer packages – which students can access according to their needs. The centre may also provide equipment such as closed-circuit television.

Role Playing is a means of rehearsing acquired skills or testing out possible solutions to a problem, generally in relation to people, in a 'safe' environment. It can be used in two-person situations such as selection interviewing or discipline handling, or in larger contexts such as commercial negotiating, group decision-making, or work allocation and control. Generally it consists of acting out the situation and reflecting on behaviour, skills, and outcomes, with feedback. Role playing is seen as a valuable means of gaining greater insight into our own and other people's behaviour and motivations.

Role-Reversal A technique in which two students discuss a real, or imaginary, conflict or misunderstanding between them for a short while. They then switch chairs and personalities – A putting forward B's reasoning, and vice versa. Then they switch back and continue the discussion from their true perspective. The aim is to solve the conflict by developing greater understanding of the other point of view.

Self-Development takes place when individuals enhance their own development by accepting prime responsibility for their learning and for managing the process of learning – setting aims, making plans, choosing learning opportunities, taking full advantage of them, and evaluating outcomes. It is often assisted by a process of self-assessment, a Learning Contract (qv), access to learning resources through an Open Learning Programme (qv), or a Resource Centre (qv), and a review process of some kind.

Seminar A group learning session, with a class of maybe 8 to 12 students, plus the tutor, where the learning takes the form of the group discussion of a theory, idea, problem, etc, rather than a lecture.

Shadowing A technique in which a trainee learns managerial practice by observing and assisting ('shadowing') a manager carrying out normal tasks.

Simulation Reproduction of a real situation, in a real time frame, and in a controlled environment, to give students experience of handling realistic situations and solving realistic problems, as training for the real thing, eg flight simulation for trainee pilots.

Succession Planning is used by some organisations to ensure as far as possible that the future needs for managers are met. At their simplest, succession plans take the form of an inventory of the potential of existing managers to fill positions at various higher levels and the likelihood of that inventory being sufficient to meet anticipated needs over some agreed time period. On this basis plans can be laid to develop existing employees or to recruit others. Some organisations make very detailed plans showing who should occupy defined managerial positions in the future and which jobs certain named individuals should move to as part of their development.

Symposium A meeting at which several formal presentations on a particular subject are delivered to an audience. A commentary on the presentations is then made by another contributor as a basis for general discussion.

Syndicate Group Method A method of learning using syndicate work. A class is divided into small groups (or syndicates) of maybe six members, who work on solving the same, or related problems. Members may be assigned different roles within the syndicate, eg Chairman, Secretary, etc. Each syndicate produces a report, and these are then appraised by the class as a whole at the end of the session.

Synectics A form of group Creativity Training (qv) which encourages the development of greater creative imagination for solving theoretical or practical problems. Led by a tutor, members of a small group follow a series of structured problem-solving steps, which aim to stimulate an imaginative, irrational, emotional approach, rather than a rational, logical one. (*See also*: Brainstorming, Lateral Thinking.)

Team Building is designed to help the members of a newly formed team to accelerate the process of developing the team's identity and interacting effectively, in order to achieve high levels of present and future task performance. It generally involves a tutor or adviser working with the team on real tasks. Team building tends to be based on assumptions which derive from research on successful teams.

Tutorial A learning situation involving the tutor and a small number (up to four) of students, which enables the maximum amount of individual attention and personal interaction.

Validation A validating body is the institution that gives the degrees and diplomas and ensures that there is a comparable standard between the institutions giving the same qualifications. In the case of universities and a small number of Colleges of Higher Education validation is an internal procedure. For most Colleges of Higher Education the validating body is an external organisation such as the Open University, a local university, BTEC or SCOTVEC.

Video Feedback The use of a video recorder to enable trainees to observe their own performance (eg in interviewing, public speaking, negotiating) as an aid to assessing and modifying technique.

Helpful Agencies

All these agencies have limited resources for answering queries. You will therefore get useful help from them if your queries are very specific and if you make your query in writing. Many have useful publications.

None of them is geared to providing extensive advice to the individual on their own career and development. Some, such as IM, will provide advisory services to their own members.

IM
Institute of Management
Management House, Cottingham Road
Corby, Northants   Tel: 0536 204 222

provides a range of information, education and advisory services. A programme of short courses for managers is available on application.

BTEC
Business and Technology Education Council
Central House, Upper Woburn Place,
London WC1H 0HH   Tel: 071-413 8400

SCOTVEC
Scottish Vocational Education Council
Hanover House, 24 Douglas Street
Glasgow G2 7NG   Tel: 041-248 7900

Offers advice on vocational courses which they validate.

Organisations involved in management education and development

AMED
The Association for Management Education and Development
21 Catherine Street
London WC2B 5JS
071-497 3264

The Association for Management Education and Development is the leading voluntary association of professional individuals. It is dedicated to improving the quality and range of management education, individual and organisational development in Europe.

AMED membership is open to people who are involved in management education, training, and development such as in-company trainers and developers, human resource specialists, people responsible for management development in the public sector and in voluntary organisations, academics and consultants working in the management field. The balance between these different types of member gives AMED its unique 'bridging' role and its membership provides a richness and diversity across the different sectors and interests.

AMED is committed to striking a balance between being a learned society, a pressure group and a friendly association of individuals who work together to develop ideas and deliver superior performance based on ethical practice. Members are committed to using education and development processes which do not rely on hidden values or beliefs undisclosed to the participants.

AMED provides support and development activities for its members through its culture of concern for the individual, informality, personal challenge, and a vision based on the shared values of the need for simultaneous growth in individuals and their organisations.

AMED encourages best practice amongst its members regionally, nationally and internationally through:

- a wide range of activities throughout the year which encourage and support good ideas and practice;
- its influential publications;

- research into the processes and contexts of management education and development;
- an information network to facilitate members' contacts and range of experiences;
- the development of products and services to support members' practice and development;
- the creation of a forum for debate on management education and development issues.

BACIE   British Association for Commercial and Industrial Education
35 Harbour Exchange Square off Marsh Wall,
London E14 9GE   Tel: 071-987 8989

IPM   Institute of Personnel Management
IPM House, 35 Camp Road,
Wimbledon,
London SW19 4UX   Tel: 081-946 9100

Specialist Organisations

AMBA   Association of MBAs
15 Duncan Terrace,
London N1 8BZ   Tel: 071-837 3375

GRTA   Group Relations Training Association
Administrator: Jill Brookes,
69 Cotton Lane,
Birmingham B13 9SE   Tel: 021-449 6313

IFAL   International Foundation for Action Learning
Secretary: Krystyna Weinstein,
46 Carlton Road,
London SW14 7RJ   Tel: 081-878 7358

Book References

Institute of Management, *Management Studies Through Distance Learning*, IM factsheet.

Boak, G (1991) *Developing Managerial Competences: The Management Learning Contract*, London: Pitman.

Casey, D and Pearce, D (eds) (1977) *More Than Management Development*, Gower.

Constable, J and McCormick, R (1987) *The Making of British Managers*, BIM and CBI.

Geiger, L and Schein, V (1989) *Power and Organization Development*, Addison Wesley.

Handy, C (1987) *The Making of Managers*, National Economic Development Council.

Honey, P and Mumford, A (1986) *The Manual of Learning*, Peter Honey, Maidenhead.

Kotter, John P (1982) *The General Managers*, Free Press.

Local Government Training Board *Going for Better Management*, LGTB.

Mintzberg, H (1973) *The Nature of Managerial Work*, London: Harper & Row.

Mumford, A (1986) *Handbook of Management Development*, 2nd edition, Gower.

Nicholson, N and West, M A (1988) *Managerial Job Change: Men and Women in Transition*, Cambridge University Press.

Pedler, M (ed) (1983) *Action Learning in Practice*, Gower.

Pedler, M, Burgoyne, J and Boydell, T (1986) *A Manager's Guide to Self-Development*, 2nd edition, McGraw Hill.

Peters, R J and Waterman, R H (1982) *In Search of Excellence*, London: Harper & Row.

Jane Skinner and Rennie Fritchie (1988) *Working Choices: A Life-planning Guide for Women Today*, London: Dent.

Winfield, M (1990) *Minding Your Own Business*, London: Social Audit, p 4.

Woodcock, M and Francis, D (1982) *The Unblocked Manager: a Practical Guide to Self-development*. Gower.

Index